Operating Systems Quiz Book

A compendium of over 1,600 short questions with answers

S.R. Subramanya

Exskillence
San Diego, USA

Table of Contents

Preface

Operating systems are central to any computing system. They manage the resources in a computing system – the processor(s), memory (RAM), devices, file system, and network interfaces. They strive to balance numerous activities, ensure efficient use of resources in a safe manner, and provide a seamless, convenient, and effective interface for users to utilize the computing system. Modern computing systems have a wide range of capabilities and purposes. For example, the smartphones, tablets, laptops, desktops, servers, and mainframe computers all share a common fundamental underlying architecture – the von Neumann architecture. They all have operating systems of varying capabilities, but share fundamental characteristics, objectives, functionalities, and modules, despite several idiosyncratic features in proprietary operating systems. A course in operating systems theory and principles is one of the fundamental/core courses in any Computer Science program. For professionals in computing/IT and related areas, knowledge of operating systems is essential at one or more levels ranging from user level to system level.

For students who are taking a course on Operating Systems, or have already taken this course, or have otherwise learnt the topics of this course, there are not many comprehensive resources for a quick assessment/testing of the fundamental understanding of the principles, concepts, and techniques of operating systems. This book aims to fill that need. It has over 1,600 short questions with answers, covering all the major topics in a typical operating systems course. For details of the solution to any question, there are numerous textbooks and Web resources.

This is a quick assessment book / quiz book. It has a vast collection of a wide variety of questions on Operating Systems. The book covers questions on the operating systems structures, fundamentals of processes and threads, CPU (processor) scheduling, process synchronization, deadlocks, memory management, I/O subsystem, and mass storage (disk) structures.

Unique features of this book

- Over 1,600 short questions, with answers.
- Questions are of only two types – True/False and sentence completion.
- All questions are single sentence and have consistent format.
- Questions have a wide range of difficulty levels.
- Questions are designed to test a thorough understanding of the topical material.
- Questions also cover popular ones asked in internship / job interviews.

Who could benefit from this book?

- Students who are currently taking Operating Systems course could use this book for self–assessment and to focus on topics one is unsure about. This helps in improving the performance in tests and exams.
- Students who have already finished a course in Operating Systems, and are preparing to take written exams and/or interviews for industry/companies.
- Faculty can use it as a resource to quickly select a few questions as part of a quiz being prepared.
- Professionals trying to make a switch to Computing/IT industry could use it as a source of self–assessment.
- Interviewers / Managers / Technical leads could use it to make a quick assessment of the candidates' fundamental understanding of OS concepts, in phone / personal interviews.
- Participants and quiz masters in quiz competitions may draw upon the vast pool of questions/answers.

Notes

- The terms 'Concurrent processes' and 'Cooperating processes' are used synonymously.
- A single core CPU is assumed, unless otherwise specified.
- Modules, structures, and functionalities of contemporary operating systems are assumed.
- The memory pages/frames are assumed to be byte addressable.
- The terms 'page table' and 'page map table' are used synonymously.
- The questions in each topical section are not necessarily in particular order.
- Occasionally (although rarely) a question is phrased in multiple ways.
- Multiple-choice questions (MCQs) have not been used on purpose.
- Questions cover topics of fundamental nature which are common to all modern/contemporary operating systems.
- Features specific to any proprietary operating system are not used in the questions.

Questions

(True/False)

A. Introduction and OS structure

A1   On power up, the bootstrap program is first run. _____

A2   The bootstrap loader brings the *entire* operating system into memory. _____

A3   The kernel initializes the CPU registers, device controllers, and memory. _____

A4   The entire operating system (such as Linux) will fit in the main memory. _____

A5   Most systems store only a small portion of the bootstrap loader program in the ROM/EEPROM. _____

A6   The operating system kernel consists of all system and application programs in a computer. _____

A7   Flash memory is slower than DRAM but needs no power to retain its contents. _____

A8   A *boot block* cannot be more than just one physical sector. _____

A9   A *command interpreter* is an example of a systems program. _____

A10   A *Web browser* is an example of a systems program. _____

A11   Location of boot blocks on the disk are not fixed. _____

A12   Most modern operating systems provide support for symmetric multiprocessing (SMP). _____

A13   All of Operating System needs to be in memory for proper execution. _____

A14   A program, as an executable file residing on disk, is static. _____

A15   System programs are part of the kernel. _____

A16   System programs are associated with the operating system.
_____

A17   Application programs are not associated with the operating of the system. _____

A18   An initial small bootstrap program is located in the random-access memory (RAM). _____

A19   Most modern operating systems are implemented (coded) using a high-level language. _____

A20   Code / software to control I/O devices is (usually) not part of the operating system. _____

A21   Not all parts of an operating system can be implemented in a high-level language. _____

A22   Implementing the operating system in a high-level language facilitates portability. _____

A23   It is possible to run applications which are larger than can fit in the physical memory (RAM). _____

A24   Main Memory (RAM) is volatile memory. _____

A25   An operating system supporting more than one processor is called multiprogramming. _____

A26   Multiprogramming increases CPU utilization. _____

A27   Turning off interrupts can be done in user mode. _____

A28   Reading the system clock can be done in user mode. _____

A29   User programs can set the mode bit. _____

A30   All of Operating System needs to be in memory for proper execution. _____

A31   User programs can set the mode bit. _____

A32   A multicore system allows two (or more) threads that are in compute cycles to execute at the same time. _____

A33   In an SMP-type system each processor performs all tasks within the operating system. _____

A34   In a peer-to-peer systems, clients may sometimes act as servers. _____

A35   Kernel supported threads can be scheduled independently. _____

A36   The microkernel approach facilitates ease of extending the operating system. _____

A37   In the microkernel approach, addition of new services requires modification of the kernel. _____

A38   The microkernel approach facilitates ease of portability of the operating system. _____

A39   In the microkernel approach, all new services are added to user space. _____

A40   The microkernel approach, most services run as kernel services. _____

A41   The microkernel approach does not provide more security and reliability. _____

A42   Shared memory is better suited to IPC (inter-process communication) mechanism than message passing for distributed systems. _____

A43   A message-passing model is faster than the shared memory model. _____

A44   A message-passing model is better suited than a shared memory model for communication between computers. _____

A45   CPU executes with very limited capability in user mode. _____

A46   A system call is initiated by hardware. _____

A47   Mechanisms for process synchronization are provided by the operating system. _____

A48 The entire executable code of a process need not reside in memory (RAM). _____

A49 The OS strives to keep the CPU running all the time. _____

A50 The entire operating system must reside in the memory (RAM) for correct operation. _____

A51 A job mix with more I/O-bound processes than compute-bound processes has (comparatively) lower CPU utilization. _____

A52 System calls are usually invoked by using software interrupts. _____

A53 Application programmers typically use an API rather than directory invoking system calls. _____

A54 Shared memory is typically faster than message passing. _____

A55 Message passing is typically faster than shared memory. _____

A56 Message passing is better suited compared to shared memory for exchanging large amounts of data. _____

A57 The operating system in a modern single user PC/laptop is not a multiprogramming OS. _____

A58 In a modern single user PC/laptop several processes will be running even when the user has no running programs/applications. _____

A59 The microkernel communicates with devices. _____

A60 A microkernel provides only inter-process communication and access control. _____

A61 Applications divided into separate tasks can run in parallel on the different cores. _____

A62 In multicore systems data must also be divided to make them accessible by the tasks running on separate cores. _____

A63   A *multiprogramming* system must have more than one CPU.
_____

A64   A *multiprocessing* (or *multiprocessor*) system must have two or more processors. _____

A65   Even a single user system (such as desktop or laptop) is a *multiprogramming* system. _____

A66   Concurrency is only possible with parallelism. _____

A67   The CPU checks for a pending interrupt at the end of every few instructions. _____

A68   The CPU checks the interrupt line at the end of every instruction.
_____

A69   At the end of every instruction, the CPU checks to see if the interrupt line is asserted. _____

A70   In a multiprogramming OS, the CPU *waits* for I/O of a process to complete before resuming execution. _____

A71   A real-time process may get a disproportionate share of the resources. _____

A72   The CPU will not use all the features provided by the hardware while executing in user mode. _____

A73   A *trap* instruction switches the execution mode of a CPU from user mode to kernel mode. _____

A74   All interrupts result in context switches. _____

A75   All context switches are due to interrupts. _____

A76   *Context switch* time does not affect the overall performance.
_____

A77   A *non-preemptive* kernel is essentially free from race conditions.
_____

A78   A thread making a change to a shared global variable is visible to other cooperating threads. _____

A79   Starting addresses of exception handlers are also (usually) stored in the same table as those of interrupt handlers. _____

A80   An *interrupt* could be caused by a condition within a processor. _____

A81   Concurrent execution of processes/threads must require multiple processors/cores. _____

A82   A process modifying a kernel data structure can be interrupted. _____

A83   Modification of a kernel data structure cannot be done in user mode. _____

A84   Interrupts can have different priorities. _____

A85   CPU switches to kernel mode upon any interrupt or exception. _____

A86   Dynamic loading facilitates better memory utilization. _____

A87   With dynamic loading the entire program does not have to be stored in main memory. _____

A88   Normal programs run at a level above the lowest interrupt priority. _____

A89   Attempt to execute an illegal instruction generates an interrupt. _____

A90   Some interrupt handlers are run in user mode. _____

A91   Too many context switches would adversely affect the throughput. _____

A92   Handling (processing) of any interrupt is never interrupted. _____

A93   The kernel/user mode bit can be set by the user process. _____

A94   An executable program is always loaded in the same memory location at every invocation. _____

A95   The bootstrap program is typically larger than one disk block.
       _____

A96   Interrupts generated by devices are given higher priority than traps
       generated by the user program. _____

A97   Code used for handling system calls can never be interrupted.
       _____

A98   A faster CPU may not always ensure improved CPU utilization.
       _____

A99   Increasing the degree of multiprogramming always improved the
       CPU utilization. _____

A100   The check for a pending interrupt is done at the end of finishing
       every instruction. _____

A101   *Aging* is used to ensure that jobs in the lower-level queues will
       eventually complete their execution. _____

A102   A context switch takes place at every system call. _____

A103   A reentrant program cannot be called recursively. _____

A104   Parts of reentrant code can be altered during execution. _____

A105   A multiprogramming operating system must have more than one
       CPU. _____

A106   The degree of multiprogramming is the number of processes in
       the ready queue. _____

A107   Before proceeding to execution of the interrupt service routine
       (ISR), the OS disables interrupts. _____

A108   Shared memory is a preferred method of communication when
       processes are in two different machines. _____

A109   Providing APIs (Applications Programmer Interface) to system
       calls facilitate portability of programs across systems. _____

A110   Accessing an out-of-bounds memory location causes an interrupt.
       _____

A111 Interrupts are disabled while running an interrupt service routine (ISR). _____

A112 Static (non-shared) libraries can be linked with object files before run-time. _____

A113 There are no additional run-time loading costs for non-shared (static) libraries. _____

A114 Traps can be generated intentionally by a user program. _____

A115 User programs have no control over when an interrupt occurs. _____

A116 Increasing the degree of multiprogramming results in increased CPU utilization. _____

A117 A high level of CPU utilization and a low level of disk usage calls for reduction of the degree of multiprogramming. _____

A118 An executable program is never in main memory (RAM) unless it has been invoked (started). _____

A119 A process (a program that has been invoked) is always in main memory and *never* present on the disk. _____

A120 Access to a memory location which is out of bounds for the process causes an interrupt. _____

A121 Attempt to execute an illegal instruction (OP code) causes an exception (trap). _____

A122 System calls can be run in either user mode or kernel mode. _____

A123 Issuing a trap instruction can happen in user mode. _____

A124 Turning off interrupts can be done in user mode. _____

A125 Switching from user to kernel mode must be done in kernel (supervisory) mode. _____

A126 Attempt to perform an illegal memory access causes an interrupt. _____

A127   Attempt to execute an illegal instruction causes a trap. _____

A128   Most systems ignore some interrupts in order to allow a critical instruction to execute without interruption. _____

A129   It is possible to create a thread library without any kernel-level support. _____

A130   A multicore system allows two (or more) threads that are in compute cycles to execute at the same time. _____

A131   Relocation register is used to check for invalid memory addresses generated by a CPU. _____

A132   With the use of interrupt mechanism, the processor has to wait for the duration of I/O, without executing instructions from any other process. _____

A133   Increasing the main memory (RAM) size (generally) improves the CPU utilization. _____

A134   There is no instruction that cannot be interrupted. _____

A135   A multi-core system requires each core to have its own cache memory. _____

A136   A message-passing model is easier to implement than a shared memory model for inter-computer communication. _____

A137   The message passing is faster than shared memory for communication between computers/processors. _____

A138   System calls can sometimes be run in either user mode. _____

A139   Message passing is more commonly used for exchanging large amounts of data. _____

A140   Upon an interrupt, a running processes never goes to waiting state. _____

A141   Degree of multiprogramming refers to the number of cores in a CPU. _____

A142   The degree of multiprogramming increases with increase in memory (RAM). _____

A143   A process cannot be moved from one memory location to another during execution. _____

A144   Dynamic linked libraries (DLLs) link to an application at compile time. _____

A145   Dynamic linked library (DLL) is loaded onto RAM and run only as needed. _____

B. Processes and threads

B1   The parent and child processes never share (a segment of) memory. _____

B2   The kernel has knowledge of user-level threads. _____

B3   Every user-level thread must belong to a process. _____

B4   Every kernel-level thread need not be associated with a process. _____

B5   Two or more processes cannot be concurrently running the same executable program. _____

B6   A context switch can never be voluntary (initiated by the running process). _____

B7   A process in user mode cannot execute certain privileged hardware instructions. _____

B8   Termination of a running process will always result in context switch. _____

B9   A timer interrupt will result in involuntary context switch. _____

B10   The context switch happening to a process due to an interrupt is considered voluntary. _____

B11   A process will have a context switch every time it enters kernel mode from user mode. _____

B12   A context switch always results in swapping. _____

B13   A running process requesting an I/O operation results in a context switch. _____

B14   Upon a page fault a process always blocks. _____

B15   A page fault always results in swapping out of a page. _____

B16   The clock interrupt can never be disabled. _____

B17   It is possible for a process to go directly from *waiting* state to *running* state. _____

B18   A running process can never go to the *ready* state without first going to the *waiting* state. _____

B19   It is possible for a process to go directly from *ready* state to *finished* state. _____

B20   A process can never go to the *waiting* state from the *ready* state. _____

B21   A process could go to the *finished* state from *waiting* state. _____

B22   A process can never go to the *running* state from the *ready* state. _____

B23   A process can never go to the *finished* state from the *waiting* state. _____

B24   A process always goes to the *ready* state from the *waiting* state. _____

B25   A process can never go to the *finished* state from the *ready* state. _____

B26   A process could go to the *running* state from the *waiting* state. _____

B27   A process can never go to the *running* state from the *waiting* state. _____

B28   A process always go to the *finished* state from the *running* state. _____

B29   An executing process must be in memory (RAM). _____

B30   A process not currently executing, but in ready state, need not be in memory (RAM). _____

B31   After the **fork()** system call, the parent process and the child process share the data, stack and heap areas. _____

B32   A traditional (or heavyweight) process has a single thread of control. _____

B33   A thread is composed of a thread ID, program counter, register set, and heap. _____

B34   Each thread has its own register set and stack. _____

B35   A benefit of a thread pool is to reduce the overhead of repeated thread creation. _____

B36   It is possible to create a thread library without any kernel-level support. _____

B37   Thread Libraries provide APIs for creating and managing user-level threads. _____

B38   Different user-level threads of a process can be scheduled to run on separate processors. _____

B39   The kernel manages user-level threads. _____

B40   Every user-level thread is associated with a process. _____

B41   The kernel manages only the kernel-level threads. _____

B42   Multiple user-level threads on a multiprocessor system provide better performance than on a single-processor system. _____

B43   When a kernel thread blocks inside the kernel it could be swapped out. _____

B44   Multiple kernel-level threads can be run on multiple processors. _____

B45   With the number of kernel threads equal to the number of processors, the processors are guaranteed to be kept busy all the time. _____

B46   In a single CPU system, multiple processes can be in the *waiting* state. _____

B47   In a single CPU system, only one process can be in the *running* state. _____

B48   In a single CPU system, only one process can be in the *ready* state. _____

B49   In a single CPU multiprogramming system, multiple processes can be executing at any time. _____

B50   In a single CPU multiprogramming system, multiple processes can be resident in memory at any time. _____

B51   In a single CPU system, multiple processes can be in the waiting state at the same time. _____

B52   It is possible for a process to go directly to the *running* state from *waiting* state. _____

B53   Upon interrupt by a higher priority process, the process in *running* state goes to *waiting* state. _____

B54   Lengths of the subsequent CPU bursts of processes are known exactly in advance. _____

B55   The program in *reentrant code* cannot be shared among processes. _____

B56   The data in *reentrant code* can be shared among processes. _____

B57   Heap memory and global variables are shared among the threads of a multithreaded process. _____

B58   In a single CPU system, only one process can be in the *running* state. _____

B59   In a single CPU system, only one process can be in the *ready* state. _____

B60   Two *independent* processes can affect each other. _____

B61   Shared–memory is a means of inter–process communication. _____

B62   After the **fork()** system call, the parent process and the child process share the data, stack and heap areas. _____

B63   Each process executes its own *critical section*. _____

B64   After the **fork()** system call, the parent process and the child process share the data, stack and heap areas. _____

B65   The kernel manages only the kernel-level threads. _____

B66   Switching between user level threads requires kernel intervention. _____

B67   Kernel threads are slower to create and manage compared to user threads. _____

B68   In the *many-to-one* model, multiple user threads can access the kernel at the same time. _____

B69   In the *many-to-one* model, the entire process will not block if a thread makes a blocking system call. _____

B70   In the *many-to-one* model, multiple threads are unable to run in parallel on multiprocessors. _____

B71   The *many-to-one* model provides more concurrency than the *one-to-one* model. _____

B72   In the *one-to-one* model, another (user) thread can run when a (user) thread makes a blocking system call. _____

B73   In the *many-to-many* model, N user level threads can map to more than N user level threads. _____

B74   In the *many-to-many* model, N user level threads cannot map to less than N user level threads. _____

B75   In the *one-to-one* model, multiple threads are unable to run in parallel on multiprocessors. _____

B76   In the *many-to-many* model, multiple threads are able to run in parallel on multiprocessors. _____

B77   Implementing inter-process communication is easier than implementing inter-thread communication. _____

B78 A process goes from the running state to the ready state when an interrupt occurs. _____

B79 Threads cannot use their own stack, other than that of the parent. _____

B80 A thread cannot have its own program counter. _____

B81 A thread has the same address space as its process. _____

B82 Threads of the same process can share the same stack. _____

B83 Each process can have its own address space. _____

B84 A process may span multiple pages. _____

B85 After a process spawns a child process, the parent and child continue to execute the same set of instructions from that point onwards. _____

B86 After a process spawns a child process, the order of execution of the instructions in the parent and child processes is indeterminate. _____

B87 Just after a child process is created, is a duplicate of the parent. _____

B88 Just after a child process is created, it does not run concurrently with the parent. _____

B89 After a child process is created, it usually has a new program loaded into it. _____

B90 A newly admitted process will be in running state. _____

B91 In the *many-to-one* mapping of user threads to kernel threads, if one user thread blocks, the other threads belonging to the same process can continue to run. _____

B92 In the *one-to-one* mapping of user threads to kernel threads, there is a working set for each thread of a multi-threaded process. _____

B93   After an I/O event is completed, a process goes to *running* state.
_____

B94   After an I/O event is completed, a process goes to *terminated* state.
_____

B95   Switching threads causes a trap to the kernel. _____

B96   Even if one user level thread of a process blocks, the entire process blocks. _____

B97   If one kernel level thread of a process blocks, another thread can continue execution. _____

B98   Management of user level threads is done by the kernel. _____

B99   Switching between user and kernel modes takes more time than switching between two processes. _____

B100   Communication between processors on a multi-core chip is faster than processors on separate chips. _____

B101   A process may completely be residing on the disk (secondary memory). _____

B102   A process must always reside in main memory (RAM). _____

B103   Contemporary operating systems support kernel threads. _____

B104   Kernel threads are generally no more expensive to maintain than user threads. _____

B105   Kernel threads need not be associated with a process. _____

B106   A web server a typically run as a single-threaded process.
_____

B107   A web server that runs as a single-threaded process can serve only one client. _____

B108   A multithreaded program can allow the program to run even if part of it is blocked. _____

B109　The threads of a process do not share the resources belonging to the process. _____

B110　Multiple user-level threads of a process can run on multiple processors. _____

B111　A thread can be run on any processor when multiple processors are available. _____

B112　Multiple kernel-level threads of the same process can run on multiple processors simultaneously. _____

B113　A thread library could be implemented to reside in user space or kernel space. _____

B114　A kernel-level thread library is supported directly by the operating system. _____

B115　A kernel-level thread library the code and data structures exist in kernel space. _____

B116　A thread pool avoids the overhead of repeated creation of new threads. _____

B117　The code, data, and files are shared across the threads of the same process. _____

B118　The threads of a process share the set of registers and the stack. _____

B119　Stack is not shared by threads of the same process. _____

B120　A thread cannot have its own stack, other than that of the parent process. _____

B121　All threads of a process share the same code. _____

B122　All threads of a process do not share the same data. _____

B123　Blocking one kernel level thread blocks all related threads. _____

B124　More memory requested (dynamically) by a running process is allocated on the stack. _____

B125   Kernel support is required for the creation and destruction of user-level threads. _____

B126   A process that is waiting for an event to occur must necessarily do a spinlock. _____

B127   When a process does a spinlock, there will necessarily be a context switch. _____

B128   A process waiting in some waiting queue for an event to occur will not expend CPU time. _____

B129   Aging involves gradually increasing the priority of a process. _____

B130   In a livelock situation, a process will eventually get to run on the CPU. _____

B131   Use of aging allows a low priority process to use the CPU in the presence of higher priority processes. _____

B132   Interrupt processing is done in user mode. _____

B133   An interrupt is *never* deferred. _____

B134   Even in a single user system, multiple processes could be in different states of execution at any time. _____

B135   Traps can be generated due to some effects of instruction executions within a process. _____

B136   The interrupted process is always *immediately* resumed after servicing the interrupt. _____

B137   A thread can be scheduled and executed independently of its parent process. _____

B138   Multithreaded programs facilitate increase of CPU usage. _____

B139   A thread may sometimes be run on only a selected processor even when multiple processors are available. _____

B140 The time taken to switch between user and kernel modes of execution is less than the context switch time. _____

B141 Allocating a process all its resources before beginning its execution improves resource utilization. _____

B142 A kernel thread does not have its own address space. _____

B143 Thread-specific data generated by the thread is independent of the thread's process. _____

B144 The OS does not maintain a separate stack for each thread. _____

B145 Context switch is faster with kernel-supported threads. _____

B146 Switching among threads (of the same process) is no more efficient than switching among processes. _____

B147 A high-priority process which is ready, would never have to wait while a low-priority process is running. _____

B148 After an I/O event is completed, a process goes to the *running* state. _____

B149 Several processes can be running in kernel mode. _____

B150 Most modern operating systems swap entire processes to swap space. _____

C. CPU Scheduling

C1   Typically the scheduler gives higher preference to CPU-bound processes to run on the CPU compared to I/O-bound processes.
_____

C2   Typically the I/O-bound processes do not use up their quantum of time. _____

C3   The CPU bursts of compute-bound processes are typically larger than those of I/O-bound processes. _____

C4   Having I/O-bound processes use the CPU ahead of compute-bound processes reduces the average wait time of processes.
_____

C5   Reducing the context-switch frequency tends to increase the average response time of processes. _____

C6   Reducing the context-switch frequency tends to decrease the CPU utilization. _____

C7   The SJF scheduling could lead to starvation. _____

C8   The RR scheduling could lead to starvation. _____

C9   The RR scheduling is non-preemptive. _____

C10   The RR scheduling could lead to starvation. _____

C11   The permanent assignment of a process to a particular queue in a multilevel feedback-queue system provides more flexibility.
_____

C12   A process entering a multilevel feedback queue is usually placed in the (lower priority) FCFS queue. _____

C13   The Shortest Job First (SJF) scheduling could lead to starvation.
_____

C14   The Shortest Job First (SJF) scheduling is non-preemptive.
_____

C15   The Shortest Remaining Time (SRT) scheduling is non-preemptive. _____

C16   The RR scheduling could lead to starvation. _____

C17   The RR scheduling is non-preemptive. _____

C18   The FCFS scheduling scheme will never lead to starvation. _____

C19   The Shortest Job First (SJF) scheduling would not lead to starvation. _____

C20   The RR scheduling will never lead to starvation. _____

C21   In RR scheduling, a running job can never be interrupted. _____

C22   In Round-robin (RR) scheduling, the time-quantum should be small with respect to the context-switch time. _____

C23   The most complex scheduling algorithm is the multilevel feedback-queue algorithm. _____

C24   Round-robin (RR) scheduling degenerates to first-come-first-served (FCFS) scheduling if the time-quantum is too long. _____

C25   The FCFS scheduling scheme could lead to starvation. _____

C26   CPU bursts are predicted based on past behavior (CPU usage pattern). _____

C27   The different levels of a multilevel queue system must have the same time-quantum. _____

C28   Scheduling with larger time-quantum generally requires fewer context switches. _____

C29   A high priority process in a real–time system runs in non–preemptive mode. _____

C30   Starvation is not an issue in priority scheduling. _____

C31   Starvation is an issue in round robin (RR) scheduling. _____

C32   Starvation is not an issue in first-come-first-served (FCFS) scheduling. _____

C33   Starvation is not an issue in shortest job first scheduling. _____

C34   Starvation is an issue in shortest remaining time first scheduling. _____

C35   Priority scheduling gives the minimum average waiting time. _____

C36   Shortest job first (SJF) scheduling gives the minimum average waiting time. _____

C37   Multiple-level queues is not really a separate scheduling algorithm. _____

C38   Shortest remaining time (SRT) is a non-preemptive process scheduling algorithm. _____

C39   Earliest deadline first (EDF) is a preemptive process scheduling algorithm. _____

C40   The long-term scheduler selects a *mix* of CPU-bound and I/O-bound jobs. _____

C41   Short (CPU time) processes are disadvantaged in FCFS scheduling. _____

C42   In round-robin scheduling jobs can get different quanta of time. _____

C43   In round-robin scheduling, the time-quantum should be large compared to context switch time. _____

C44   Round-robin scheduling is not well suited for real-time systems. _____

C45   FCFS scheduling is well suited for real-time systems. _____

C46   Preemptive scheduling is well suited for real-time systems. _____

C47   Preemptive scheduling may cause starvation. _____

C48   Shortest remaining time first scheduling will not cause starvation. _____

C49   FCFS provides better response time than round robin scheduling. _____

C50   Increasing the time-quantum would result in decreased average turnaround time. _____

C51   Increasing the time-quantum would result in increased average waiting time. _____

C52   In non–preemptive scheduling, *every* process runs to completion without being taken out of the CPU. _____

C53   In multilevel queue scheduling, a newly entering process is placed in the *lowest priority* queue. _____

C54   In non-preemptive scheduling a process can continue to run till it finishes execution. _____

C55   In non-preemptive scheduling a process can continue to run till it finishes with its current CPU burst. _____

C56   Each of the queues in multi-level feedback queue scheduling must have the same scheduling algorithm. _____

C57   A multi-level feedback queue scheduler generally assigns a long quantum to low priority processes. _____

C58   In round robin (RR) scheduling, when the quantum is small, there will be more context switches. _____

C59   *Convoy effect* can happen only in non–preemptive scheduling. _____

C60   *Convoy effect* can happen even in preemptive scheduling. _____

C61   In multilevel queue scheduling, processes can move between queues. _____

C62   Processes can move across queues in a multilevel feedback queue system. _____

C63   The context switch overhead increases when the RR time-quantum is increased. _____

C64   The terms *process scheduler* and *CPU scheduler* refer to different things. _____

C65   The CPU scheduler is not present in a single CPU system. _____

C66   In preemptive scheduling, the sections of code affected by interrupts must be guarded from simultaneous use. _____

C67   Process scheduler can move a job from running to waiting state. _____

C68   In a single CPU system, the *first in first out* scheduling results in the minimum average waiting time. _____

C69   Increasing the time-quantum in round-robin CPU scheduling, always results in increased turn-around time. _____

C70   Preemption is a 'must' for interactive systems. _____

C71   While switching context from process A to process B, the process A is always swapped out. _____

C72   The CPU scheduler can interrupt a running process. _____

C73   In *Little's formula*, λ represents the average waiting time in the queue. _____

C74   Predicting the next CPU burst of processes is not relevant in first-come-first-served(FCFS) scheduling. _____

C75   Predicting the next CPU burst of processes is needed in round robin (RR) scheduling. _____

D. Process synchronization

D1   Race condition refers to the indeterminate nature of the order of executions of a set of (assembly/machine language) statements.
_____

D2   Synchronization among cooperative processes is necessitated by data sharing. _____

D3   Use of semaphores, no matter in what order the programmer uses, guarantee proper synchronization. _____

D4   Semaphores are used for controlled access to both critical section as well as to shared resources. _____

D5   The *entry section* ensures that the conditions are right for the process to enter it's *critical section*. _____

D6   Each of the cooperating processes has its own *critical section*.
_____

D7   *Binary semaphores* cannot be used for the critical-section problem for multiple processes. _____

D8   Race condition can occur only in multiprocessor systems.
_____

D9   Race conditions are prevented by requiring that critical regions be protected by locks. _____

D10   All solutions to the critical section problem are based on some form of locking. _____

D11   Multiple processes can be executing their critical sections at the same time. _____

D12   The *Test-and-Set* instruction should be executed atomically (without interruption). _____

D13   The *semaphore* used for synchronization of two (or more) processes need not be a shared variable. _____

D14   In a normal system, more than one of concurrent processes could execute in their *critical regions*. _____

D15   Synchronization of concurrent processes may not guarantee the same (consistent) results when executed at different times. _____

D16   Synchronization is not required among concurrent processes which do not share resources. _____

D17   A *semaphore* is essentially an integer variable. _____

D18   A semaphore can be modified simultaneously by multiple threads. _____

D19   A semaphore is a shared variable (memory location). _____

D20   Semaphores cannot provide the same functionality as mutex locks. _____

D21   A process typically spends a small percentage of its time in its critical section. _____

D22   The variable shared among cooperating processes is accessed/updated in the *critical section*. _____

D23   Each of the concurrent cooperating processes has its own *critical section*. _____

D24   The value of *any* semaphore can range only between 0 and 1. _____

D25   Process *starvation* is not possible while using semaphores. _____

D26   In the *Readers–Writers* problem, more than one reader can be reading simultaneously. _____

D27   In the *readers–writers* problem, the semaphore that ensures mutual exclusion between the writer and reader processes must be a counting semaphore. _____

D28   A counting semaphore can never be used as a binary semaphore. _____

D29   A binary semaphore can never be used as a counting semaphore.
_____

D30   A counting semaphore can be simulated using multiple binary
semaphores. _____

D31   Spinlocks can be used to prevent busy waiting in the
implementation of semaphore. _____

D32   Counting semaphores can be used to control access to a resource
with a finite number of instances. _____

D33   A semaphore can be used to control access to a thread's critical
sections. _____

D34   The value of a counting semaphore can range only between 0 and
1. _____

D35   The local variables of a monitor can be accessed by only the local
procedures. _____

D36   The semaphore in the producer–consumer problem which controls
access to the shared buffer could be a binary semaphore.
_____

D37   The semaphore used to ensure mutual exclusive access to critical
section by two (or more) processes need not be a shared variable.
_____

D38   The exact order of executions of statements of concurrent
processes could be different when executed at different times.
_____

D39   Even with synchronization, concurrent processes could produce
different results when executed at different times. _____

D40   Synchronization of concurrent processes guarantees the same
(consistent) results even when executed at different times.
_____

D41   A process typically spends a small percentage of its time in its
critical region. _____

D42 A binary semaphore can be used when there is no more than one resource. _____

D43 Semaphores can be simulated using monitors. _____

D44 Monitors cannot be simulated using semaphores. _____

D45 A binary semaphore which is initialized to 1 will never be negative when working properly. _____

D46 If a process using a binary semaphore invokes the **signal** operation in its entry section, and the **wait** operation in its exit section, multiple processes could be in their critical sections.

_____

D47 If a process using a binary semaphore invokes the **wait** operation in its entry section, and the **wait** operation in its exit section, none of the other processes could be in their critical sections. _____

D48 In a system with two processes P_1 and P_2, and a binary semaphore, S used for accessing a critical section, if P_2 is missing **signal(S)**, then P_1 can still enter its critical section. _____

D49 In a system with two processes P_1 and P_2, and a binary semaphore, S used for accessing a critical section, if P_2 is missing **signal(S)**, then P_2 cannot enter its critical section the second time around. _____

D50 In a system with two concurrent processes $P1$ and $P2$ synchronized using a binary semaphore S, when $P2$ is in its critical section, $P1$ cannot be in its exit section. _____

D51 In a system with two concurrent processes $P1$ and $P2$ synchronized using a binary semaphore S, when $P2$ is in its critical section, $P1$ can be in its entry section. _____

D52 In a system with two concurrent processes $P1$ and $P2$ synchronized using a binary semaphore S, when $P2$ is in its critical section, $P1$ can be in its remainder section. _____

D53   In a system with two concurrent processes *P1* and *P2* synchronized using a binary semaphore *S*, when *P2* is in its critical section, *P1* can be in its critical section. _____

D54   In a system with two concurrent processes *P1* and *P2* synchronized using a binary semaphore *S*, when *P1* is in its entry section, *P2* can be in its entry section. _____

D55   In a system with two concurrent processes *P1* and *P2* synchronized using a binary semaphore *S*, when *P1* is in its exit section, *P2* cannot be in its entry section. _____

D56   In a system with two concurrent processes *P1* and *P2* synchronized using a binary semaphore *S*, when *P1* is in its exit section, *P2* can be in its exit section. _____

D57   In a system with two concurrent processes *P1* and *P2* synchronized using a binary semaphore *S*, when *P1* is in its remainder section, *P2* can be in its remainder section. _____

D58   Process *deadlock* is a possibility while using semaphores. _____

D59   The *semaphore* used to ensure mutual exclusive access to critical section by two (or more) processes need not be a shared variable. _____

D60   The semaphore used for synchronization must be a shared variable. _____

D61   In the *readers–writers* problem, each reader process has exclusive access to the buffer. _____

D62   In the *readers–writers* problem, the reader and writer processes have exclusive access to the buffer. _____

D63   In the *readers–writers* problem, multiple reader processes can access the buffer. _____

D64   A critical section can consist of multiple instructions. _____

D65   The producer-consumer problem cannot be solved using monitors. _____

D66   The producer-consumer problem can be solved *only* using semaphores. _____

D67   Only a subset of the instructions in a critical section are executed as an atomic unit (without interruption). _____

D68   Semaphore value is modified in the *remainder* section of the code. _____

D69   A semaphore need not be updated in a mutually exclusive manner. _____

D70   A binary semaphore cannot be used to implement mutual exclusion among N processes. _____

D71   Mutual exclusion is optional for non–sharable resources. _____

D72   Mutual exclusion is required for all sharable resources. _____

D73   Mutual exclusion is not required for some sharable resources. _____

D74   Switching the order of execution of *wait()* and *signal()* in a process will always result in deadlock. _____

D75   Switching the order of execution of *wait()* and *signal()* in a process will affect mutual exclusion. _____

D76   Switching the order of execution of *wait()* and *signal()* in a process could result in several processes to be active in their critical sections at the same time. _____

D77   Giving preference to multiple readers to access the shared resource (buffer) versus a single writer, increases the throughput in the *readers-writers* problem. _____

D78   The number of licenses in commercial software packages indicating the number of applications that may run concurrently, can be implemented using a semaphore. _____

D79   A critical section can never be nested inside another one. _____

D80   In a set of cooperating processes, no assumptions may be made about speeds of the processes. _____

D81   In a set of cooperating processes, more than one process cannot be in its critical section. _____

D82   Using the monitor construct, only one process at a time can be active within the monitor. _____

D83   A *monitor* is an object whose methods are always executed in mutual exclusion. _____

D84   The variable shared across cooperating processes is updated in the *critical section*. _____

D85   Cooperating processes share a common critical section. _____

D86   Peterson's solution would work for synchronization of more than two processes. _____

D87   Each process executes its own *critical section*. _____

D88   Two independent processes can affect each other. _____

D89   Shared–memory is a means of inter–process communication. _____

D90   Allowing several threads try to access (read) the same data concurrently is allowed in many applications. _____

D91   An instruction which is said to execute atomically must consist of only one machine instruction. _____

D92   Processes that are executing in their critical sections can participate to decide on the next process to enter its critical section. _____

D93   Race conditions are prevented by requiring that critical sections be protected by locks. _____

D94   The *semaphore* used to ensure mutual exclusive access to critical section by two (or more) processes need not be a shared variable. _____

D95   The *critical section* is shared among cooperating processes. _____

D96   Semaphores used by cooperating processes must be global variables. _____

D97   Operations on semaphores must be done atomically. _____

D98   When a process starts spinlock, it continues to use the CPU. _____

D99   Mutex locks and counting semaphores are equivalent. _____

D100 Mutex locks and binary semaphores are equivalent. _____

D101 A process modifies the value(s) of semaphore(s) in the critical section. _____

D102 Mutual exclusion will not be affected if the semaphore operations (wait and signal) are not done atomically. _____

D103 The operations on a semaphore must be done atomically (mutually exclusively). _____

D104 Multiple mutually disjoint processes have no need for synchronization. _____

D105 Accesses (reads) to files and databases by cooperating processes must always be mutually exclusive. _____

D106 Updates (writes) to files and databases by cooperating processes need not always be mutually exclusive. _____

D107 A process can access/update shared data in its entry section. _____

D108 The *test-and-set* instruction must execute uninterrupted for correct operation. _____

D109 The *test-and-set* instruction is a single machine level instruction. _____

D110 A lock that uses busy wait is called a *spinlock*. _____

D111 *Busy wait* is a hindrance to efficient use of CPU. _____

D112 Busy waiting can be avoided by having the processes waiting on a semaphore to enter a *blocked* state. _____

D113 A spinlock is useful when locks are expected to be held for long amounts of time. _____

D114 The local variables of a monitor can be accessed by only the local procedures. _____

D115 Spinlocks waste CPU cycles. _____

D116 Spinlocks are not appropriate for single-processor systems. _____

D117 Bulk of the work of a process is done in the *critical section*. _____

D118 The data streamed from a Web server to a client fits the *readers-writers* model. _____

D119 Cooperative clients accessing a database fits the producer-consumer model. _____

D120 Critical regions protected by locks prevents race conditions. _____

D121 *Mutual exclusion* is not a necessary condition for deadlock. _____

D122 *Hold and wait* is a necessary condition for deadlock. _____

D123 *No preemption* is not a necessary condition for deadlock. _____

D124 The *banker's algorithm* is useful in a system with single instance of each resource type. _____

E. Deadlocks

E1   Excessive resource usage is not a necessary condition for deadlock. _____

E2   In a system which is in an unsafe state, it is possible for the processes to complete their executions without getting into a deadlock. _____

E3   The circular-wait condition for a deadlock implies the hold-and-wait condition. _____

E4   Prevention is most commonly used in practice for handing deadlocks. _____

E5   Despite allocation of all of a job's required resources, it may still cause deadlock. _____

E6   Removal of any one of the four necessary conditions for deadlock prevents deadlock. _____

E7   If there is no circular wait (for resources) a deadlock can still occur. _____

E8   When a system is in the unsafe state, it will eventually lead to deadlock. _____

E9   A deadlock avoidance system may, at times, allow the system to enter the unsafe state. _____

E10   The total number of existing resources could be less than the total demands of all the processes and still maintain safety. _____

E11   Deadlock avoidance is less restrictive than deadlock prevention. _____

E12   A cycle in the resource-allocation graph with only one instance of every resource type does not necessarily indicate a deadlock situation. _____

E13   A job may hold onto a resource even after finishing. _____

E14   Allocation of even only a subset of the required resources to processes could lead to deadlock. _____

E15   Allocation of all of the required resources to a process may not lead to deadlock. _____

E16   *All* of the four necessary conditions for deadlock must be removed for deadlock prevention. _____

E17   A circular wait for resources is not necessarily a deadlock situation. _____

E18   Deadlocks can be prevented by not allowing at least one of the four necessary conditions. _____

E19   The wait-for graph scheme is not applicable to a resource allocation system with multiple instances of each resource type. _____

E20   The *banker's algorithm* is applicable in a system with multiple instances of each resource type. _____

E21   Deadlock prevention and deadlock avoidance are essentially the same approaches for handling deadlock. _____

E22   Excessive resource usage can cause deadlock. _____

E23   A safe state may lead to a deadlocked state. _____

E24   A safe state will never lead to a deadlocked state. _____

E25   An unsafe state is always a deadlocked state. _____

E26   If there is no circular wait (for resources) a deadlock can still occur. _____

E27   Deadlock prevention and avoidance are the same thing for handling deadlocks. _____

E28   A system in an unsafe state will eventually deadlock. _____

E29   Deadlock avoidance requires knowledge of resource requirements a priori. _____

E30 With only a single shared resource, a deadlock situation will not occur. _____

E31 All *starvation* situations are due to *deadlocks*. _____

E32 Database records could be shared resources. _____

E33 Not allocating partial list of the resources for a process may result in reduced performance. _____

E34 It is always possible to know in advance the resource requirements of every process. _____

E35 Breaking a deadlock always requires at least one victim process (to be terminated). _____

E36 Deadlock is not possible while the system is in a safe state. _____

E37 Deadlock cannot occur with spooled resources. _____

E38 A *safe state* ensures that there is a sequence for processes to finish their program execution. _____

E39 In an unsafe state there are no free resources in the system. _____

E40 Existence of more than zero free resources in the system guarantees that it is safe state. _____

E41 Removal of 'hold and wait' condition requires processes to request all the resources needed before starting. _____

E42 Removal of 'hold and wait' condition will not reduce the efficiency of use of resources. _____

E43 Releasing all resources before requesting a new resource is a valid deadlock prevention scheme. _____

E44 Starting execution only after obtaining all required resources will not result in the deadlock of that process. _____

E45   Circular wait is avoided by assigning precedence to resources and requiring processes to request resources in order of increasing precedence. _____

E46   Disabling interrupts during critical sections will not avoid circular waits. _____

E47   A deadlock-avoidance scheme facilitates more concurrent use of resources than schemes that statically prevent deadlock formation (deadlock prevention). _____

E48   A deadlock-avoidance scheme will not contribute to increased runtime overheads. _____

E49   When the CPU wants to perform a memory read/write, it is *always* granted immediate access to memory bus. _____

E50   Imposing a total ordering of all resource types and requiring the resources to be acquired in order, prevents deadlock from occurring. _____

E51   Requiring a process to request resources only when it has none, will ensure *hold-and-wait* condition never occurs. _____

E52   Requiring a process to request all its resources before the start of its execution may not guarantee that *hold-and-wait* condition never occurs. _____

E53   Imposing a total ordering of all resource types and requiring the resources to be acquired in order, may not guarantee absence of circular-wait condition. _____

E54   In practice, the deadlock-detection algorithm is invoked for every resource request. _____

E55   Deadlock is still possible while the system is in a safe state. _____

E56   Assigning a resource to a process which is in safe state may take it to an unsafe state. _____

E57   A process is in a deadlocked state whenever it is waiting for resources that are being used by other process(es). _____

E58   Circular wait is a necessary, but not sufficient condition for deadlock. _____

E59   Preempting a resource is a deadlock recovery mechanism. _____

E60   Killing one of the processes is a deadlock recovery mechanism. _____

E61   A cycle in the resource-allocation graph is a necessary and sufficient condition for deadlock in the case where each resource has more than one instance. _____

E62   A cycle in the resource-allocation graph is a necessary and sufficient condition for deadlock in the case where each resource has exactly one instance. _____

E63   The circular-wait condition for deadlock implies the hold-and-wait condition. _____

E64   In a system where each resource type contains only a single instance and the resource-allocation graph contain cycles, a deadlock exists. _____

E65   In case of a resource type containing more than one instance, the presence of a cycle in the resource-allocation graph does not guarantee deadlock. _____

E66   Not all unsafe states lead to deadlocks. _____

E67   In a deadlocked system, a job/process which is not deadlocked could never be chosen as the victim to be terminated. _____

E68   If a system does not have deadlocks, it is guaranteed not to have starvation. _____

E69   If a system has multiple cooperating processes, but only one shared resource then it will not have deadlocks. _____

E70   Deadlock would not occur if the number of resources is greater than the number of processes. _____

E71   If there are no cycles in the resource allocation graph, then there is no deadlock. _____

E72   If there are cycles in the resource allocation graph, then there is deadlock. _____

E73   Presence of a cycle in a *wait-for* graph indicates deadlock. _____

E74   A safe state ensures that there is a sequence of processes to finish their program execution. _____

E75   A process which is deadlocked is necessarily starved. _____

E76   A process which is not deadlocked is never starved. _____

E77   When a system has no available free resources, then it is in a deadlock state. _____

E78   When a system is in deadlock state, it has no available free resources. _____

E79   In practice, systems are designed for deadlocks never to occur. _____

E80   Deadlocks *never* need manual intervention. _____

E81   A deadlock-free solution eliminates the possibility of starvation. _____

E82   In the *Dining Philosophers* problem with 5 philosophers, 3 of them may eat simultaneously. _____

E83   If a resource-allocation graph has a cycle, the system must be in a deadlocked state. _____

E84   Schemes for preventing hold-and-wait conditions also prevent starvation. _____

E85   A deadlock-free solution eliminates the possibility of starvation. _____

E86   In the case of each resource having exactly one instance, a cycle in a resource-allocation graph is a necessary and sufficient condition for a deadlock. _____

E87   In the case of each resource having more than one instance, a cycle in a resource-allocation graph is a necessary and sufficient condition for a deadlock. _____

E88   The *wait-for* graph scheme is not applicable to a resource allocation system with multiple instances of each resource type. _____

E89   The *wait-for graph* can be used only in the case of a single instance of each resource type. _____

E90   Deadlocked processes can come out of deadlocked state without external intervention. _____

E91   A system with no available free resources always indicates a deadlocked condition. _____

E92   Hold and wait is not a sufficient condition for deadlock. _____

E93   No preemption is not a sufficient condition for deadlock. _____

E94   Unsafe state is a subset of deadlock state. _____

E95   Removal of any one condition (out of the four) is removed, the deadlock will be resolved. _____

E96   The *Banker's algorithm* is used for prevention of deadlocks. _____

E97   Multithreaded programs are not prone to deadlocks. _____

E98   Allocating a process all its resources before beginning its execution avoids deadlocks. _____

E99   Defining a linear ordering of resource types prevents circular wait. _____

E100   Circular wait is not a sufficient condition for deadlock. _____

E101   Mutual exclusion is not a sufficient condition for deadlock. _____

F. Memory management and virtual memory

F1   Under contiguous allocation, a running process requesting more memory (dynamically) may result in relocation of the entire process. _____

F2   Under pure segmentation, a running process requesting more memory (dynamically) may not result in relocation of the entire process. _____

F3   The contiguous memory allocation scheme does not allow processes to share code. _____

F4   The segmentation scheme does not allow processes to share code. _____

F5   The paging scheme does not allow processes to share code. _____

F6   Paging suffers from external fragmentation. _____

F7   The relocation register is used to check for invalid memory addresses generated by a CPU. _____

F8   The physical address space is smaller than logical (virtual) address space. _____

F9   Arithmetic/Logic operations can be directly performed by the CPU on memory contents. _____

F10   Cache memory could be as large as the main memory (RAM). _____

F11   The base and limit registers ensure the validity of the addresses of a process. _____

F12   The relocation register is used to obtain the physical memory addresses. _____

F13   The Best-Fit allocation scheme minimizes internal fragmentation. _____

F14　Paging has external fragmentation. _____

F15　Segmentation has external fragmentation. _____

F16　Segmentation has no internal fragmentation. _____

F17　The First-Fit allocation scheme takes a longer time to look for a free block compared to others. _____

F18　The logical address space is generally much larger than the physical address space. _____

F19　The sizes of (logical) pages and (physical) frames are different. _____

F20　The higher order bits of the logical address representing the page number are used to directly index the Page Table to get the frame number. _____

F21　The offset of a byte within a page is the same as the offset of the byte within the frame to which the page maps. _____

F22　The first-fit allocation method generally finds a partition faster than the best-fit allocation. _____

F23　The best-fit allocation method need not search for all the free blocks before an allocation. _____

F24　The first-fit allocation method must search for all the free blocks before an allocation. _____

F25　All the pages of a program/job/process need not be of the same size. _____

F26　The page size and the main memory frame size are of the same size. _____

F27　All the pages of a job/process must always reside in the main memory. _____

F28　All the pages of a job/process are always stored in contiguous main memory frames. _____

F29   A smaller page size results in a correspondingly larger page table. _____

F30   There are as many page tables as there are jobs/processes. _____

F31   The average memory access time decreases with increase in cache hit ratio. _____

F32   The byte offset within a memory frame is the same as the byte offset in the corresponding page. _____

F33   The number of entries (rows) in a page map table depends on the number of pages in the job. _____

F34   The CPU could sometimes bypass the cache and access the memory (RAM) directly. _____

F35   There is a *job table* for every active job in the system. _____

F36   The (page map table) PMT (or part of it) also resides in (some part of) main memory. _____

F37   There are situations when the PMT may not contain the frame numbers for some pages. _____

F38   In a PMT (Page Map Table) entry, if the *modified* field/bit is not set, then corresponding page is not written onto disk. _____

F39   The contents of the PMT can never change during the lifetime of a job. _____

F40   Pages of a given process (job) may have different sizes. _____

F41   All page map tables (PMTs) are of the same size. _____

F42   Each job/process has its own page map table. _____

F43   All memory frames in a system are of the same size. _____

F44   There are as many entries (rows) in a page map table as there are memory frames. _____

F45   The PMT contains the memory frame number for *every* page of a job/process. _____

F46   Cache memory can sometimes be as big as the main memory (RAM). _____

F47   Increasing the number of page frames in main memory may not reduce page faults across all page replacement algorithms. _____

F48   Increasing the number of page frames in main memory always reduces page faults under FIFO page replacement algorithms. _____

F49   There is one *valid-invalid* bit per page of logical memory. _____

F50   Optimal page replacement is the preferred page-replacement used in practice. _____

F51   Optimal page replacement algorithm keeps track of previously used pages. _____

F52   Optimal page replacement algorithm is impossible to implement. _____

F53   Optimal page replacement algorithm assumes a 'knowledge' of the future. _____

F54   Optimal page replacement is used as a benchmark for performance of page replacement schemes. _____

F55   Segments can sometimes be paged. _____

F56   Segmented paging is helpful when the page table is small. _____

F57   When large contiguous sections of the page table are unused, they can be collapsed into a single-segment table entry. _____

F58   Sharing a reentrant module is easier using segmentation than using pure paging. _____

F59   Multiple pages are never mapped onto the same hashed page table entry. _____

F60   The byte offset within the mapped frame is the same as the byte offset in the corresponding virtual page. _____

F61   The byte offset within the mapped frame could be different than the byte offset in the corresponding virtual page. _____

F62   Each entry of the TLB contains the (logical) page number and the corresponding (physical) frame number. _____

F63   The number of TLB entries depends on the (logical) page size. _____

F64   The number of TLB entries depends on the (physical) frame size. _____

F65   The number of TLB entries is independent of the logical address space. _____

F66   A process always blocks on a TLB miss. _____

F67   A page reference might have a TLB miss but no necessarily a page fault. _____

F68   The frame number from a page table is obtained by using the page number as an index into the page table. _____

F69   The number of entries in a page table depends on the number of (logical) pages. _____

F70   The number of entries in a page table depends on the number of (physical) frames. _____

F71   A page cannot be in main memory (RAM) if that page number is not in TLB. _____

F72   The number of entries in a TLB depends on the number of pages. _____

F73   The TLB entries are sorted by the virtual page numbers. _____

F74   In a TLB all the entries need to be searched sequentially.
_____

F75   A page fault must be preceded by a TLB miss. _____

F76   A TLB miss always indicates page fault condition. _____

F77   In a TLB, all the entries are searched sequentially. _____

F78   Context switching time is typically much less than swap in/out time. _____

F79   Fragmentation does not occur in a paging system. _____

F80   On a demand-paging system, a process will experience a high page fault rate when the process begins execution. _____

F81   The page table entries are the addresses of frames in physical memory. _____

F82   Reference to a page that is not residing in main memory causes an interrupt. _____

F83   Segmentation has fixed-sized blocks. _____

F84   In paged segmentation, there are multiple memory references per page. _____

F85   Each process has its own page table. _____

F86   Inverted Page Table contains one entry per physical page frame.
_____

F87   The number of entries in an *inverted* page table depends on the number of logical pages. _____

F88   Address translation under segmentation requires just two registers per segment. _____

F89   Segmentation has higher memory overhead in the logical to physical address translation compared to paging. _____

F90   In pure paging, the page table only has as many entries as there are pages of the process in the main memory. _____

F91   In pure paging, the page table spans all of the virtual address space of the program. _____

F92   Two processes having the same number of bits of logical address, but with different number of page requirements have page tables of different sizes. _____

F93   Programs which require more memory than is available in physical memory cannot be run. _____

F94   Loading only the necessary pages for execution of a process into memory will have no effect on the I/O overhead for swapping. _____

F95   Demand paging increases the degree of multiprogramming. _____

F96   In pure demand paging, the page fault rate is initially high. _____

F97   Not requiring all of the pages of a process to be in memory increases the throughput. _____

F98   Paged segmentation reduces wasted memory due to external fragmentation. _____

F99   Paged segmentation reduces memory allocation time. _____

F100   It is easier to share a reentrant module using paging than when using segmentation. _____

F101   There cannot be a page fault when there is a TLB hit. _____

F102   There is always a page fault when there is a TLB miss. _____

F103   A TLB miss always results in the process being blocked. _____

F104   The page table contents do not change at context switch. _____

F105   The translation look-aside buffer (TLB) contents change at context switch. _____

F106   Some pages of a process may be heavily used, while some rarely (or not at all). _____

F107   The least recently used (LRU) is not (computationally) expensive to implement. _____

F108   Extra hardware is required for the efficient implementation the LRU algorithm. _____

F109   Trashing can also be a consequence of poor page replacement algorithms. _____

F110   There is a separate inverted page table for every process. _____

F111   Inverted page table stores the paging information of all the processes in a single table. _____

F112   An inverted page table stores one entry per physical frame. _____

F113   Very small page size is the likely cause of trashing. _____

F114   Far too many processes running in a system is likely cause of trashing. _____

F115   Virtual memory increases the degree of multiprogramming. _____

F116   Increasing the memory (RAM) of a system typically helps reduce the page fault rate. _____

F117   A large virtual address space and a small page size results in a small page table size. _____

F118   The minimum number of page frames that must be allocated to a running process is determined by physical memory size. _____

F119   A multi-level page table helps reduce the number of page faults. _____

F120   A multi-level page table reduces the effective memory access time. _____

F121   Every process has its own TLB. _____

F122   On a context switch, the TLB is saved on the stack. _____

F123   Every page entry in TLB has the corresponding page residing in a physical (main memory) frame. _____

F124   Every page residing in a physical (main memory) frame, may not have an entry in the TLB. _____

F125   Smaller page size results in larger page table size. _____

F126   Smaller page sizes result in larger internal fragmentation. _____

F127   Larger page sizes (generally) tend to reduce page faults. _____

F128   The entire memory image of a process must be moved from memory to disk during swap out. _____

F129   Only selected pages of a process in memory frames are moved from memory to disk during swap out. _____

F130   Repopulating the TLB could be a significant component of context switching. _____

F131   On a context switch, all the entries of a tagged TLB are invalidated. _____

F132   Hashed page tables are commonly used for handling addresses larger than 32 bits. _____

F133   The TLB (irrespective of any additional data) must always be flushed during a context switch. _____

F134   The size of the page table is independent of the size of the virtual address space. _____

F135   A larger virtual address space would have a larger page table. _____

F136   Entries in the segment table of two different jobs can never point to the same physical location. _____

F137   A segment could belong to the address space of two different processes. _____

F138   Lower order bits of logical address give the page number. _____

F139   More than one (physical) frame can correspond to a given (logical) page. _____

F140   While using segmentation, the segments may be of variable length. _____

F141   Using segmentation, the segments must be allocated contiguously. _____

F142   Segmentation does not suffer from external fragmentation. _____

F143   A large page table can itself be paged. _____

F144   A page selected for swapping out is *always* written on disk. _____

F145   Page table entries of two or more different processes may never have the same page number when those processes are active. _____

F146   The design principles of the TLB are similar to those of cache. _____

F147   The TLB is usually organized as fully-associative cache. _____

F148   Multiple processes share the TLB. _____

F149   With larger page size, the page table size will be correspondingly larger. _____

F150   A process is never prevented from reading or writing some of its own memory. _____

F151   It is always the case that every page of a process is brought into main memory (at some point) during the execution of a process. _____

F152   A process is always permitted to read or write some of its own memory. _____

F153   When the bit in a page table entry is set to 'valid', this value indicates that the associated page is both legal and in memory. _____

F154   If a page is valid but not in memory, the valid/invalid bit in the page table entry would be set to 'valid'. _____

F155   The *offset* in the logical address must always be less than the *limit* field of the segment table entry. _____

F156   An *offset* in the logical address which is greater than the *limit* field of the segment table entry generates a page fault. _____

F157   The most frequently used page always causes the most number of page faults. _____

F158   The most frequently used page always causes the least number of page faults. _____

F159   The least frequently used page always causes the most number of page faults. _____

F160   The least frequently used page always causes the least number of page faults. _____

F161   In general, virtual memory decreases the degree of multiprogramming in a system. _____

F162   A process with too many frames will likely have a high page-fault rate. _____

F163   A page selected for replacement needs to be *always* written to disk. _____

F164   Prepaging reduces the initial page fault rates. _____

F165   Implementation of associative memory requires hardware support. _____

F166   Increasing the TLB reach by increasing the TLB size is expensive (due to high associate memory cost). _____

F167 Increasing TLB reach by increasing the page size is not a common practical approach. _____

F168 The virtual memory can be (theoretically) as large as the secondary (disk) memory size. _____

F169 Increasing the number of entries in the TLB increases the TLB reach. _____

F170 Increasing the page size will not increase the TLB reach. _____

F171 A process with more pages will always experience more page faults than one with lesser pages. _____

F172 The number of page faults experienced by a process is independent of its access patterns of instructions and data. _____

F173 A thread always blocks on a TLB miss. _____

F174 A thread may continue to run on a TLB miss. _____

F175 Checking for the read / write privileges while accessing a page is (usually) done in hardware. _____

F176 There is one inverted page table entry for every logical page. _____

F177 There are as many inverted page table entries as there are physical frames. _____

F178 The search time in an inverted page table is less than that of a normal page table. _____

F179 In a *hashed* page table, no two page numbers can ever hash to the same entry. _____

F180 The TLB contains only a subset of the page table entries. _____

F181 A page number which is not found in the TLB always results in page fault. _____

F182   The physical address space of a process has to be contiguous.
_____

F183   A process being swapped in has to be brought to the same memory frames it occupied before being swapped out. _____

F184   The fundamental working of *paging* is dependent on temporal and spatial locality of programs. _____

F185   The fundamental working of *cache* is not dependent on temporal and spatial locality of programs. _____

F186   Each entry in the page table contains a bit that indicates if the virtual page is actually mapped to a physical frame. _____

F187   All the locations in an associative memory can be looked up in constant time. _____

F188   Separate caches are always needed for instructions and data.
_____

F189   The *first-fit* memory allocation method results in the least fragmentation. _____

F190   Segmented memory allocation will not have internal fragmentation. _____

F191   The unit of transfer between cache and main memory must equal a word or an addressable unit. _____

F192   Each page table entry contains the (logical) page number in addition to the (physical) frame number. _____

F193   The K–way set-associate mapping refers to having K sets of cache lines. _____

F194   Cache line size could be different from the main memory block size. _____

F195   There is a 1:1 correspondence between the number of TLB entries and the number of page table entries. _____

F196   Hashed page tables are particularly useful for processes with sparse address spaces. _____

F197 Inverted page tables require each process to have its own page table. _____

F198 Each entry of the TLB contains the (logical) page number and the corresponding (physical) frame number. _____

F199 The number of entries in a TLB depends on the number of pages. _____

F200 The TLB entries are sorted by the virtual page numbers. _____

F201 In a TLB all the entries need to be searched sequentially. _____

F202 Reducing the page size results in increase in the number of TLB entries. _____

F203 The page table can also be swapped out to disk occasionally. _____

F204 The inverted page table saves space compared to a normal page table. _____

F205 Segmentation has fixed-sized blocks. _____

F206 Page table entry contains both the page number and the frame number. _____

F207 TLB entry does not contain the logical page number. _____

F208 In a direct–mapped cache, the cache replacement algorithms are not applicable. _____

F209 The order of bytes (or words) in a main memory block and those in the corresponding cache line are the same. _____

F210 A process can modify its own address translation table(s). _____

F211 The byte offset for an object in physical frame need not be the same as the byte offset in the corresponding logical page. _____

F212 Parts of logical memory space of a process may be occupied by the some pages of the operating system. _____

F213 In the partition scheme of memory allocation, the size of each process must be less than the physical memory size. _____

F214 A TLB hit for a page access guarantees no page fault (for that access). _____

F215 The *first-fit* memory allocation method suffers from external fragmentation. _____

F216 The *best-fit* memory allocation method does not suffer from external fragmentation. _____

F217 The TLB helps in reducing the access to page tables during address translation. _____

F218 The TLB entries are searched sequentially. _____

F219 The number of TLB entries will be equal to the number of pages in a process. _____

F220 There will be one system-wide TLB. _____

F221 A multilevel page table reduces the size of page table (compared to single-level page table). _____

F222 A multilevel page table reduces the number of page faults (compared to single-level page table). _____

F223 Page table is looked up only after a TLB miss. _____

F224 Memory protection is usually done by the processor and associated hardware. _____

F225 A segment table must always fit within a page. _____

F226 Page fault rate has no effect on effective memory access time. _____

F227 Cache hit ratio has an effect on effective memory access time. _____

F228   The hash values in the entries of a hashed page table correspond to (physical) frame numbers. _____

F229   The FIFO page replacement algorithm could suffer from *Belady's* anomaly. _____

F230   All reference strings (access patterns) using FIFO exhibit *Belady's* anomaly. _____

F231   The *second-chance* algorithm does not suffer from *Belady's* anomaly. _____

F232   Stack algorithms can never exhibit *Belady's* anomaly. _____

F233   Least recently used (LRU) page replacement algorithm does not suffer from *Belady's* anomaly. _____

F234   Distributing heavily used pages evenly over all of memory would reduce page faults. _____

F235   Memory protection is not needed in a single user system. _____

F236   In paged memory systems, increase of page size reduces the internal fragmentation. _____

F237   Page fault cannot occur while trying to store (write) data in memory (RAM). _____

F238   The FIFO page replacement algorithm is the one implemented on most systems. _____

F239   Any instruction or data access really requires two memory (RAM) accesses. _____

F240   A process cannot have more than one working set. _____

F241   A program having good locality of reference would have less page faults. _____

F242   In a system supporting virtual memory, portions of multiple programs may reside in memory at the same time. _____

F243 Demand paging works on the principle that only portions of a program are needed / are active in a short time window. _____

F244 There is no requirement of minimum number of page frames that must be allocated to a running process in a virtual memory environment. _____

F245 Every page selected to be swapped out need not be written onto disk. _____

F246 CPU generates physical address (of RAM) during execution. _____

F247 It is *never* the case that the same (logical) page number of two different processes in the system map to the same (physical) frame number. _____

F248 Cache data transfers are done in blocks. _____

F249 Under-allocation of pages for processes causes trashing. _____

F250 Trashing has no effect on CPU utilization. _____

F251 Increasing the degree of multiprogramming could reduce trashing. _____

F252 The CPU generates physical memory (RAM) addresses when executing instructions of a process. _____

F253 CPU accessing a data item in a page which is not in any memory frame (RAM) causes an interrupt. _____

F254 When significant time is spent in paging, decreasing the degree of multiprogramming improves the CPU utilization. _____

G. I/O subsystem

G1   Spooling facilitates overlapping of I/O and CPU operations. _____

G2   An interrupt is a hardware-generated event. _____

G3   During DMA data transfer, the CPU just waits for the I/O to complete. _____

G4   Using DMA, the data transfer between memory and I/O device, and CPU execution can proceed simultaneously. _____

G5   There is one common queue for all devices in a system. _____

G6   Direct Memory Access (DMA) is not suitable for slow (ex. keyboard, mouse) devices. _____

G7   Direct Memory Access (DMA) is used for any I/O device. _____

G8   Direct Memory Access (DMA) is suitable for high speed devices doing bulk data transfers. _____

G9   Use of memory-mapped I/O to device control registers eliminates the need for special I/O instructions. _____

G10   In memory-mapped I/O, user programs can access memory addresses associated with the device control registers. _____

G11   Buffering is not needed with mouse devices. _____

G12   Interrupt-driven I/O is not suitable for mouse input. _____

G13   Interrupt-driven I/O is suitable for keyboard input. _____

G14   Polling is used only for input devices. _____

G15   Polling is not needed in memory-mapped devices. _____

G16   Interrupts are not needed in memory-mapped devices. _____

G17 Interrupts are used only for data transfers from the device to the memory (input device). _____

G18 Non-blocking I/O is better suited to mouse and keyboard input. _____

G19 Non-blocking I/O is better suited when the order of I/O arrival from multiple devices is not predetermined. _____

G20 Interrupt-driven I/O is less efficient than busy waiting (in terms of CPU utilization). _____

G21 When the DMA controller is using the memory bus for data transfer, the CPU waits if it needs to use of the bus. _____

G22 Interrupt-driven I/O is more efficient than polling under any circumstance. _____

G23 When I/O is frequent and of short duration, polling is efficient. _____

G24 I/O operations (typically) take place synchronously with respect to the CPU. _____

G25 All kinds of I/O requests by a process will result in the process getting transitioned to waiting state. _____

G26 During a DMA I/O transfer, if the CPU wants to do a memory access, the DMA transfer is paused. _____

G27 Notification of completion of I/O transfer is done via a trap (exception). _____

G28 Memory-mapped I/O can be used only with an interrupt-driven device driver. _____

G29 Memory-mapped I/O can be used with a polling-based device driver. _____

G30 The I/O module is the interface between the CPU and the peripheral device. _____

G31 In programmed I/O, the CPU is tied up during a data transfer from the device to I/O module. _____

G32   Drivers are specific to a given operating-system. _____

G33   CPU is actively involved in DMA mode data transfer. _____

G34   In DMA transfer, an interrupt is generated for every byte of transfer. _____

G35   The CPU has to continuously monitor the DMA I/O transfers. _____

G36   The device controller communicates directly with the operating system. _____

G37   Direct memory access (DMA) is not suitable for all devices. _____

G38   Some devices combine both polling and interrupts. _____

G39   In *polling*, the CPU must periodically scan (read) an address to check if an input has arrived. _____

G40   The CPU will be waiting while the DMA systems transfers data between memory and I/O device. _____

G41   In busy wait mode of I/O, the CPU will be waiting for I/O to complete. _____

G42   Interrupts are due to events that occur outside of processor execution. _____

G43   Every keyboard click may not cause an interrupt. _____

G44   A device completing an I/O operation generates a trap. _____

G45   There are different drivers for a given device for different operating systems. _____

G46   For CPUs having explicit I/O instructions, I/O protection can also be ensured by executing the I/O instructions in user mode. _____

G47   When I/O is frequent and of short duration interrupt-driven I/O is not efficient. _____

H. Secondary (disk) storage and file system

H1   Higher speed disk drives (compared to lower speed ones) do not necessarily improve the rotational latency. _____

H2   In general, LOOK disk head scheduling will involve less movement of the disk heads than SCAN disk head scheduling. _____

H3   The outer track of platter in a disk drive has more sectors than the inner track(s). _____

H4   All the sectors on a given track are not of the same size. _____

H5   The sectors on different tracks of a magnetic disk are of the same (physical) size. _____

H6   Every sector, irrespective of the track, contains the same amount of data. _____

H7   Rotational delay (search time) is the slowest of the three components of disk I/O. _____

H8   In movable head disk drives, the read/write heads of different platters could be on different tracks. _____

H9   In fixed–head disk drives, the seek time is the slowest component of disk I/O. _____

H10   The track(s) of platters of magnetic disk drives are spiral. _____

H11   Seek time depends on the disk's RPM. _____

H12   Rotational latency (delay) is independent of the disk's RPM. _____

H13   With constant angular velocity disk drive, the same amount of data is under the head across all tracks. _____

H14   With constant angular velocity disk drive, the storage density decreases going from outside to inside. _____

H15   With constant angular velocity disk drive, the number of sectors on each track decreases going from outside to inside. _____

H16   In constant linear velocity disk drive, the density of tracks increases going from outer tracks to inner tracks. _____

H17   In constant linear velocity disk drive, the density of tracks is the same across tracks. _____

H18   All files in a single-level directory must have unique names. _____

H19   A relative path name must begin at the root. _____

H20   An absolute path name must always begin at the root. _____

H21   SSTF disk scheduling algorithm may cause starvation of some requests. _____

H22   In C-SCAN algorithm, the arm moves in only one direction while servicing requests. _____

H23   The seek time of a disk drive is dependent on the rotation speed. _____

H24   The SSTF disk head scheduling algorithm does not take into account the current position of the disk head. _____

H25   The SCAN disk head scheduling algorithm does not take into account the current position of the disk head. _____

H26   Polling is inefficient for devices with unpredictable I/O operations. _____

H27   Interrupt has relatively low overhead compared to polling. _____

H28   DMA I/O operation delivers data directly to the memory of a process. _____

H29   A large fraction of the I/O software in an operating system is device dependent. _____

H30   The device driver has reentrant code. _____

H31   SCAN and C-SCAN disk scheduling algorithms could lead to starvation of request(s). _____

H32   The disk block allocation methods have no influence on the performance of disk scheduling algorithms. _____

H33   Disk controllers do not usually have a built-in cache. _____

H34   Tertiary storage is usually implemented as a jukebox of tapes or removable disks. _____

H35   The LOOK disk head scheduling offers no practical benefit over SCAN disk head scheduling. _____

H36   The LOOK disk head scheduling involves (in general) less movement of the disk heads than SCAN scheduling. _____

H37   RAID Level 1 organization achieves better performance for read requests. _____

H38   There is more overhead for the write operations on a RAID Level 5 system compared to RAID Level 1 organization. _____

H39   The throughput in the RAID system is independent of the number of disks. _____

H40   The disk scheduling algorithms could only manage the reduction of seek time. _____

H41   The rotational latency is higher than the seek time. _____

H42   In contiguous allocation, the disk head movement is minimized. _____

H43   Linked allocation of file supports direct access efficiently. _____

H44   Indexed allocation of file supports direct access efficiently. _____

H45   Disk fragmentation is avoided in linked allocation of files. _____

H46   Disk fragmentation exists in indexed allocation of files. _____

H47   Error detection is used in RAID level 0. _____

H48   RAID 0 does not use parity bits. _____

H49   In RAID, a few large-capacity disk drives are preferable to several small-capacity disk drives. _____

H50   In RAID, the data distributed across multiple disks cannot be simultaneously accessed. _____

H51   RAID level 2 provides error correction of bytes. _____

H52   RAID level 3 provides only error detection, but not error correction of sectors. _____

H53   A separate disk for parity of the blocks of other disks is used in RAID level 5. _____

H54   The parity of the blocks of the disks is spread across all the disks in RAID level 4. _____

H55   The failure of a disk can never be recovered in any RAID level. _____

H56   Potential overuse of the single parity disk can occur with RAID level 4. _____

H57   Only error detection, but not error correction is supported in RAID level 6. _____

IOIOIOIOIOIOIOIOIOIOIOIOIOIOIOIOIOIOIOIOIOIOIOIOIOI

Questions

(Sentence Completion)

A. Introduction and OS structure

A1   User programs make use of Operating System services by the use of _____

A2   _____ refers to multiple programs in various states of execution to be in the memory at the same time.

A3   The privileged instructions are executed in _____ mode.

A4   _____ stored in ROM starts up first when the machine is powered on.

A5   _____ is the bare essential kernel in which the nonessential components have been implemented as user programs.

A6   The (small) code that locates the kernel and loads it into main memory (RAM) is called _____

A7   A program that has been invoked (started) is called a _____

A8   The most common secondary storage device is _____

A9   A _____ can be used to prevent a user program from never returning control to the operating system.

A10   Embedded systems typically employ a _____ operating system.

A11   The servers may sometimes act as clients in a _____

A12   Two important design issues for cache memory are _____ and _____

A13   The bootstrap program is stored on _____

A14   A _____ combines multiple object modules into a single binary.

A15   The core (essential) part of the OS which interacts with the hardware is the _____

A16   More memory required (dynamically) by a running process is allocated on the _____ area of memory.

A17   The notion of operating system supporting than one runnable program to be in memory is called _____

A18   User programs can invoke functions in the operating system kernel by the use of _____

A19   The notion of operating system supporting than one user is called

_____

A20   Turning off (disabling) interrupts can only be done in _____ mode.

A21   Use of separate partitions of a single system to support a different operating systems is called _____

A22   A specialized computer system that is part of a larger physical system is called _____

A23   The bootstrap loader stored on ROM is also referred to as

_____

A24   The primary part of the operating system that performs the system's most essential tasks is called the _____

A25   The first (small) program to run when a computer system is powered on is the _____

A26   The bootstrap loader is resident in _____ or

_____

A27   When the bootstrap loader runs, it loads the _____ from _____ onto _____

A28   Instructions of the user programs run in _____ mode.

A29   Instructions of the OS functions run in _____ mode.

A30   The kernel mode is also called _____ or _____

A31   The mode of execution (user or kernel) is indicated by _____

A32   The address of the next instruction to be executed is contained in the _____

A33   Multiple OS environments existing simultaneously on the same machine, isolated from each other is called _____

A34   The three major queues on a typical system are _____, _____, and _____

A35   I/O-bound processes typically have _____ CPU bursts.

A36   Routines that are never used are never loaded when using _____ loading.

A37   The tiny bootstrap loader program stored in the _____ (or _____) brings the full bootstrap program from the _____

A38   Two primary models of interprocess communication are _____ and _____

A39   _____ model is better suited for communication between processors within a multiprocessor system.

A40   A kernel that is stripped of all nonessential components is called _____

A41   A _____ loads the operating system and begin its execution.

A42   Interface to the operating system services are available to user programs via _____

A43   A table of pointers to interrupt-service routines is called _____

A44   An interrupt is handled by a(n) _____

A45   A trap is handled by a(n) _____

A46   The list of starting addresses of the interrupt service routines is contained in _____

A47   User programs make use of Operating System services by the use of _____

A48   Attempt to access a memory location by a user process which has no permission, generates a ____

A49   The preferred method of process communication in a distributed system is _____

A50   Common methods used to pass parameters to the operating system during   system   calls   are   via   _____, _____, or _____

A51   In multiprocessor environments, ensuring multiple caches store the most recent version of data is called _____

A52   Interrupts are handled (processed) in _____ mode.

A53   The full bootstrap program is stored at a fixed location on the disk (partition) called the _____

A54   A software interrupt caused by an event internal to a process is called _____

A55   Before starting the interrupt service routine (ISR), interrupts are _____

A56   After finishing the interrupt service routine (ISR), interrupts are _____

A57   Modifying entries in device-status table must be done in _____ mode.

A58   An interrupt caused by software is called _____

A59   Accessing a NULL pointer causes a _____

A60   The major resources managed by the operating system are: _____, _____, _____, _____

A61 _____ is based on conditions occurring outside the processor.

A62 _____ is based on conditions occurring within the processor.

A63 The earliest the service of an interrupt can be started is _____

A64 During program execution, a divide by zero causes a(n) _____

A65 The main advantage of implementing operating systems in a high-level language is _____

A66 A computing system used in time-critical environments is called a _____

A67 Absolute code can be generated for _____ binding.

A68 The mechanism that links applications to libraries at run time is called _____

A69 The initialization of the CPU registers, device controllers, and memory is done by _____

A70 In multithreaded programs, the kernel informs an application about certain events, using a procedure known as a(n) _____

A71 The state of an interrupted process is stored in _____

A72 The entries of all the process control blocks (PCBs) of the current processes is in _____

A73 The context switch happening due to a process initiating _____ is considered voluntary.

A74   The correct sequence of actions when an interrupt occurs, among the following actions: (a) save the context of the current task in its TCB; (b) execute the ISR; (c) disable further interrupts; (d) complete the instruction that is currently being executed; (e) return to the interrupted task and continue to execute from where it left off; (f) lookup the interrupt vector to get the address of the interrupt service routine (ISR); are _____

A75   Attempt to execute an illegal instruction generates an

_____

A76   The degree of multiprogramming can be increased if the CPU utilization is _____ and the disk utilization is _____

A77   A _____ ensures that a user program always returns control to the operating system.

B. Processes and threads

B1   A _____ acts as a conduit for two processes to communicate.

B2   A _____ is an end point of communication.

B3   When a running process requests an I/O operation, the scheduler puts it in _____ state.

B4   After an I/O of a process is completed, it goes to the _____ state.

B5   Taking out a running process and bringing in another process to run is called _____

B6   The essential information of a process required by the OS is stored in the _____

B7   _____ contains the list of processes waiting for the CPU.

B8   The number of processes completed per time unit is referred to as _____

B9   A process can go to the *running* state only from _____ state.

B10 A process can go to the *terminated* state only from _____ state.

B11 A process can go to the *waiting* state only from _____ state.

B12 A blocking send() and blocking receive() is known as _____

B13 APIs for creating and managing threads is provided by _____

B14 The POSIX standard for APIs for thread creation and synchronization is called _____

B15   A _____ facilitates use of an existing thread instead of creating a new one to complete a task.

B16   The _____ model maps many user-level threads to one kernel thread.

B17   The _____ multithreading model multiplexes many user-level threads to a smaller or equal number of kernel threads.

B18   _____ is an intermediate data structure placed between user and kernel threads.

B19   The number of threads (of control) in a traditional (or heavyweight) process is _____

B20   The time that a process is expected to use the CPU continuously (without I/O) is called _____

B21   A preempted process goes from _____ to _____ state.

B22   A process requesting an I/O operation goes from _____ to _____ state.

B23   The _____ model maps each user-level thread to one kernel thread.

B24   A thread is immediately terminated in response to cancellation request in _____

B25   A thread is terminated at an appropriate time in response to cancellation request in _____

B26   _____ is a solution to the *priority inversion* problem.

B27   The situation where a high-priority process becomes ready to execute while a low-priority process is executing in its critical region is called _____

B28   The situation where a low-priority process is holding a shared resource (non-preemptively) which is required by some high-priority process is called _____

B29　The major components that are not shared across the threads of the same process are _____, _____, _____, and _____

B30　The major components that are shared across the threads of the same process are _____, _____, and _____.

B31　The creation, scheduling and management of _____ threads are done by the operating system.

B32　In the *many-to-one* model, thread management is done in _____ space.

B33　A child process which terminates without notifying the parent process is called _____

B34　A process that has terminated but has not yet released the resources is said to be in _____ state.

B35　A child process whose parent process has terminated is called

_____

B36　A thread has its own _____, _____, and

_____.

B37　After an I/O event is completed, a process goes to _____ state.

B38　When the time-quantum of an executing process expires, it goes to the _____ state.

B39　The processor could even switch threads between instructions in _____ multithreading.

B40　A thread could continue to execute on a processor until a long-latency event (ex. memory stall) occurs under _____ multithreading.

B41　The number of process control blocks (PCBs) in a system with N processes is _____

B42　The essential information pertaining to a process is stored in the OS in the _____

B43   Only from _____ state can a process go to the *finish* state.

B44   Only from _____ state can a process go to the *waiting* state.

B45   When a process executes an I/O instruction, the scheduler moves it from _____ state to _____ state.

B46   A collection of threads created at process startup is called a _____

B47   Allowing a thread to run on only a specific processor is called _____

B48   A process being moved from one area of memory to another is called _____

B49   Code that can be used by two or more processes at the same time, where executable code is shared and the data areas are separate, is called _____

B50   A program that has been invoked and is in a state of execution is called a _____

B51   The parts of the process that are shared among the threads of the same process are _____, _____, and _____

B52   Apart from the process, each of the threads have individually for themselves their own _____ and _____

B53   Saving the state of the currently running process and restoring the state of the next process to run is done at _____

B54   Completion of an I/O event transitions the process to _____ state.

B55   Two primary means of inter-process communication are _____ and _____

B56   Having more than one thread sharing the process address space is called _____

B57   After an I/O event is completed, a process goes to the _____ state.

B58   Multiple threads of a process communicate using _____

B59   The basic categories of threads are _____ threads and _____ threads.

B60   Temporary data such as local variables, function parameters, and return addresses of process are stored in the _____

B61   Information about the state of a process is contained in _____

B62   Two registers used to ensure the validity of the addresses of a process are _____ and _____ registers.

B63   The termination of all the descendants of a process being terminated is called _____

B64   A preferred method of communication when processes are in two different machines is _____

B65   Creation of several threads at process startup (even though not all of them are required) provides the benefit of _____

B66   The condition that a process is ready to run but is stuck waiting indefinitely for the CPU is called _____

B67   Degree of multiprogramming refers to the number of _____ in memory.

B68   _____ the degree of multiprogramming could reduce trashing.

C. CPU Scheduling

C1   The part of the OS that chooses processes to run on the CPU is the

_____

C2   The non–preemptive scheduling algorithm that results in the smallest average waiting time is the _____

C3   The _____ scheduling algorithm is designed especially for time-sharing systems.

C4   The lowest level of the multilevel feedback queue use the _____ scheduling.

C5   The processes with short CPU bursts are at a disadvantage in the _____ scheduling algorithm.

C6   All processes are treated fairly (equally) in the _____ scheduling algorithm.

C7   Processes with long CPU-bursts suffer starvation in the _____ scheduling algorithm.

C8   Increasing the context-switch frequency tends to _____ the average response time of processes.

C9   Increasing the context-switch frequency tends to _____ the CPU utilization.

C10   Executing the shortest tasks first _____ the average turn-around time of processes.

C11   A process may be interrupted in the middle of its execution in _____ scheduling.

C12   A process cannot be suspended before finishing its CPU burst in _____ scheduling.

C13   The two types of bursts that are used in CPU scheduler design are _____ and _____

C14   The _____ chooses processes from the ready queue to run on the CPU.

C15   The _____ scheduler decides on the swap-out
       and swap-in of processes.

C16   Predicting   the   next   CPU   burst   is   used   in   the
       _____ scheduling algorithm.

C17   _____ is a technique used to overcome starvation in
       some CPU scheduling.

C18   In multilevel queue scheduling, the _____ queue is
       partitioned into separate queues.

C19   The context switch overhead increases when the RR time-
       quantum is _____

C20   The _____ scheduler chooses processes from the
       ready queue to run on the CPU.

C21   The _____ scheduler decides on the swap-out and
       swap-in of processes.

C22   Given a set of processes with known (best estimates) of CPU
       bursts, the scheduling algorithm that gives a high throughput is

       _____

C23   In a single CPU system, the _____ scheduling
       results in the minimum average turnaround time.

C24   In a single CPU system, the _____ scheduling results
       in the minimum average waiting time.

C25   The selection of processes to be swapped out of memory is done
       by the _____ scheduler.

C26   Selection of the processes to be brought into the ready queue is
       done by _____ scheduler.

C27   Selection of the processes to be executed next (allocated CPU) is
       done by _____ scheduler.

C28   The selection of processes to be swapped into memory is done by
       the _____ scheduler.

C29   In the multi-level feedback queue system, the most often run scheduler is the _____ scheduler.

C30   An objective of the process scheduling policy is to _____ throughput.

C31   An objective of the process scheduling policy is to _____ response time.

C32   An objective of the process scheduling policy is to _____ waiting time.

C33   An objective of the process scheduling policy is to _____ turnaround time.

C34   An objective of the process scheduling policy is to _____ CPU usage.

C35   With the time-quantum in the *round-robin* (RR) policy being extremely small, each of the processes perceive the processor to be _____ than its actual speed.

C36   _____ scheduling is essentially the pre-emptive version of _____

C37   The module that gives control of the CPU to the process selected by the short-term scheduler is called _____

C38   The time taken by the dispatcher to stop one process and start another one running is called _____

C39   In FCFS scheduling, a process running with a long CPU burst, causing many processes to wait is called _____

C40   All processes are treated fairly in _____ scheduling.

C41   Turn Around Time = _____ minus _____

C42   Waiting   Time   =   _____   minus _____

C43 Compute intensive jobs are given _____ quantum of time, which results in _____ context switches.

C44 In *Little's formula*, λ represents the _____ for new processes.

C45 The second-chance algorithm is an extension of the FIFO replacement algorithm by the addition of a _____

C46 In a multi-level queue, a job which has spent significant time in the _____ queue is moved to a _____ queue.

C47 The number of processes completing their execution per time unit is called _____

C48 The time taken by a process from the time it enters the system till the time it finishes execution is called _____

C49 The amount of time a process spends without using the CPU is called _____

C50 Turnaround time is the sum of _____ and _____

C51 A technique to the solution of indefinite blockage of low-priority jobs in priority scheduling is _____

C52 Round-robin (RR) scheduling degenerates to first-come-first-served (FCFS) scheduling if the time-quantum is _____

C53 In RR scheduling with a time-quantum of Q units, and N processes in ready queue, a process (in ready queue) waits no more than _____

C54 In RR scheduling with a time-quantum of Q units, and N processes in ready queue, the average turn-around time of a process requiring T units of execution time (assuming no process goes to waiting state, and the CPU bursts of other processes is $> T$) is _____

C55 _____ is a significant problem with priority scheduling algorithms.

C56   Predicting the next CPU burst of processes is needed in
       _____ scheduling.

C57   Each queue has its own scheduling algorithm in
       _____scheduling.

C58   When the CPU scheduler picks a processes to run on the CPU
       next, it goes from _____ to _____ state.

C59   In a system of N processes, P_1, ... P_N, with CPU bursts of T_1 ...
       T_N, and $T_1 > T_2 > $ ... ... T_N, the order of arrival of the processes
       resulting in the *best* average waiting time under FCFS scheduling,
       is _____

C60   In a system of N processes, P_1, ... P_N, with CPU bursts of T_1 ...
       T_N, and $T_1 > T_2 > $ ... ... T_N, the order of arrival of the processes
       resulting in the *worst* average waiting time under FCFS
       scheduling, is _____

C61   In round robin (RR) scheduling with a quantum of Q units of time,
       and N processes with CPU bursts of T_1 ... T_N, the condition for
       every process requiring more than one timeslot to finish, is

       _____

C62   In round robin (RR) scheduling with a quantum of Q units of time,
       and N processes with CPU bursts of T_1 ... T_N, the condition for
       every process requiring no more than one timeslot to finish, is

       _____

C63   The number of processes in the ready queue in a single CPU
       system, with a total of N processes, and L of them in the waiting
       state, is _____

C64   The average turnaround time in a system of 10 processes, with the
       average waiting time is W units, and the average of the CPU burst
       times is C units, is _____ units.

C65   Given that N processes P_1, P_2, ... P_N have arrived in that order at
       some time, with CPU requirements of T_1, T_2, ... T_N, the *waiting*
       time of process P_K using FCFS scheduling is

       _____

C66   Given that N processes P_1, P_2, ... P_N have arrived in that order at some time, with CPU requirements of T_1, T_2, ... T_N, the *turnaround* time of process P_K using FCFS scheduling is

_____

C67   In multilevel queue scheduling, a newly entering process is placed in the _____ queue.

C68   In multilevel queue scheduling, a newly entering process is placed in the _____ queue (with a smaller time-quantum).

C69   In a system with 4 processes, each with a CPU burst time of 12 units, and round robin scheduling with a time slice of 5 units, the total context switches before all the processes are completed are

____

C70   In a system with four processes (which have arrived at the same time) with CPU burst times of 8, 10, 3, 7, using FCFS scheduling, the average waiting time is _____, and average turn–around time is _____

C71   In a system with four processes (which have arrived at the same time) with CPU burst times of 8, 10, 3, 7, using SJN (shortest job next), the average waiting time is ___, and average turn–around time is _____

C72   In a system with four processes (which have arrived at the same time) with CPU burst times of 8, 10, 3, 7, using RR scheduling (with a time-quantum of 2 units), the average waiting time is _____, and average turn–around time is _____

C73   In a system where three processes arrive at times 0, 1, and 3, with CPU bursts of 4, 5, and 3, the average *waiting* time using non–preemptive SJN (Shortest Job Next) scheduling, is

_____

C74   In a system where three processes arrive at times 0, 1, and 3, with CPU bursts of 4, 5, and 3, the average *turn–around* time using non–preemptive SJN (Shortest Job Next) scheduling, is

_____

C75   In a system where three processes arrive at times 0.0, 0.5, and 1.2, with CPU bursts of 4, 5, and 3, the average *waiting* time using non–preemptive SJN (Shortest Job Next) scheduling, is

_____

C76   In a system where three processes arrive at times 0.0, 0.5, and 1.2, with CPU bursts of 4, 5, and 3, the average *turn–around* time using non–preemptive SJN (Shortest Job Next) scheduling, is

_____

C77   In a system with five processes with arrival times of 0, 2, 3, 6, 10 and CPU burst times of 15, 2, 14, 10, 2, using FCFS, the average waiting time is _____, and average turn–around time is _____

C78   In a system with five processes with arrival times of 0, 2, 3, 6, 10 and CPU burst times of 15, 2, 14, 10, 2, using SJN (shortest job next), the average waiting time is _____, and average turn–around time is _____

C79   In a system with five processes with arrival times of 0, 2, 3, 6, 10 and CPU burst times of 15, 2, 14, 10, 2, using SRT (shortest remaining time), the average waiting time is _____, and average turn–around time is _____

C80   In a system with five processes with arrival times of 0, 2, 3, 6, 10 and CPU burst times of 15, 2, 14, 10, 2, using RR (with a time-quantum of 5 units), the average waiting time is _____, and average turn–around time is _____

C81   In RR scheduling with a time-quantum of 20 mS, and 5 processes in ready queue, the average turn-around time of a process requiring 305 mS of execution time (assuming no process goes to waiting state, and the CPU bursts of other processes is > 305 mS) is _____

C82   In RR scheduling with a time-quantum of 20 mS, and 5 processes in ready queue, the average turn-around time of a process requiring 290 mS of execution time (assuming no process goes to waiting state, and the CPU bursts of other processes is > 290 mS) is _____

C83   In a single CPU system with a total of N processes, W processes waiting for I/O, the number of processes in the ready queue is

_____

C84   In a system where processes issue an I/O operation every 5 milliseconds (on the average), and the context switch overhead is 0.2 milliseconds, the CPU utilization is _____

D. Process synchronization

D1   In a system with N concurrent processes, the number of possible *critical sections* is _____

D2   The _____ section is executed just before entering the critical section.

D3   The bulk of the work of a process is done in its _____ section.

D4   The number of possible values of a *binary semaphore* is _____

D5   In a concurrent system, the results of computation being indeterminate is called _____ condition.

D6   With multiple resources, a _____ semaphore is required.

D7   Binary semaphores are also called _____

D8   The busy wait of a semaphore is also called _____

D9   The number of basic operations on a semaphore is _____

D10   Updates to shared data are done by concurrent processes in their _____ sections.

D11   The two operations on a (binary) semaphore are _____ and _____

D12   In the `signal(S)` statement, the operation done on the semaphore value is _____ (or _____).

D13   The value of a counting semaphore with initial value of 10, after 6 *wait* operations and 4 *signal* operations would be _____

D14   In the *producer–consumer* problem, the _____ process has to wait when the buffer is full.

D15   In the *producer–consumer* problem, the _____ process has to wait when the buffer is empty.

D16   The _____ section precedes the critical section.

D17   The bulk of operations, other than access to shared variables, are done by a process in the _____ section.

D18   A _____ semaphore is used to synchronize the access to / use of multiple instances of a resource.

D19   In the *Dining Philosophers* problem, the _____ statement represents picking up a chopstick in the physical world.

D20   The number of writers which may concurrently share the database in the *readers-writers* problem is _____

D21   The condition where several processes (or threads) try to access and modify the same data concurrently is called

       _____

D22   The condition where outcome of execution depend on the order in which instructions are executed is called _____

D23   An instruction or a set of instructions which execute as an uninterruptible unit that that is said to execute

       _____

D24   If operations on semaphores are not done atomically, the _____ condition may be violated.

D25   In a system with N cooperating processes, the number of critical sections is _____

D26   The number of copies of a semaphore used by N cooperating processes for synchronization is ____

D27   The number of philosophers who may eat simultaneously in the *Dining Philosophers* problem with 5 philosophers is _____

D28   A process checks if can enter the critical section in the

       _____

D29   _____ are used to prevent busy waiting when implementing a semaphore.

D30   The data streamed from a Web server to a client fits the
_____ model.

D31   Cooperative   clients   accessing   a   database   fits   the
_____ model.

D32   In the classical bounded-buffer problem the number of
semaphores is _____

D33   In the classical *bounded-buffer* problem the number of binary
semaphores is _____ and the number of counting semaphores is

_____

D34   In the classical *bounded-buffer* problem the counting semaphores
indicate the _____ and _____

D35   In the classical *bounded-buffer* problem the purpose of the binary
semaphore is _____

D36   Busy waiting can be prevented when implementing a semaphore
by the use of _____

D37   The bounded-buffer is implemented as a _____

D38   In the bounded-buffer problem, the sum of the number of empty
slots and number of occupied slots in the buffer is always equal to
the _____

D39   In the readers-writers problem _____ are given
exclusive access to shared objects.

D40   A synchronization mechanism that is built into a programming
language is _____

D41   Two (or more) processes which do not affect each other during
execution are called _____ processes.

D42   Requiring a bound on the number of times that other threads are
allowed to enter their critical sections after a thread has made a
request to enter its critical section avoids _____

D43   A _____ type presents a set of programmer-defined
operations that are provided mutual exclusion within it.

D44   In a system with two cooperating processes $P1$ and $P2$ sharing a common variable named **x** with an initial value of 15, and $P1$ doing **x++** and $P2$ doing **x--**, the possible values of **x** (without any synchronization) after $P1$ and $P2$ finish execution, are

    _____

D45   A process can only access/update shared data in its

    _____

D46   In a system with two cooperating processes, a possible effect of a process calling **signal()** before entering critical section, and **wait()** after exiting critical section would be

    _____

D47   Algorithms that avoid mutual exclusion are called

    _____

D48   Concurrent accesses to _____ data without _____ may result in data inconsistency.

D49   The three requirements of a solution to the critical section problem are   _____,   _____,   and

    _____

D50   The condition where a process is prevented from execution due to waiting for resources that never become available is called

    _____

D51   The condition where the states of cooperating processes constantly change with regard to one another, but none progresses toward completion is called _____

D52   Given that the value of a counting semaphore at some instant is C, and subsequently M **wait** operations and N **signal** operations are done on the semaphore, the resulting value of the semaphore is _____

D53   Given the *producer–consumer* problem using a semaphore *mutex* (with an initial value of 1) for mutual exclusive access to the buffer, the value of *mutex* when neither producer nor consumer is in its critical section, is _____

D54   Given the *producer–consumer* problem using a semaphore *mutex* (with an initial value of 1) for mutual exclusive access to the buffer, the value of *mutex* when the producer is in its critical section, is _____

D55   Given the *producer–consumer* problem using a semaphore *mutex* (with an initial value of 1) for mutual exclusive access to the buffer, the value of *mutex* when the consumer is in its critical section, is _____

D56   Executing a loop just waiting for an event (condition) to occur is called _____

E. Deadlocks

E1   The minimum possible number of jobs required to cause deadlocks is _____

E2   The minimum possible number of resources required to cause deadlocks is _____

E3   The number of necessary conditions for a deadlock to happen is _____

E4   The *minimum* number of victim processes/jobs in order to break deadlock is _____

E5   Process P_0 waiting for a resource held by P_1, P_1 waiting for a resource held by P_2, and so on, and P_n waiting for a resource held by P_0 is referred to as _____

E6   Two or more processes waiting indefinitely for an event that can be caused by only one of the other waiting processes is known as a _____ condition.

E7   The *Banker's algorithm* is used for _____ of deadlocks.

E8   In a *safe* system, with M (L) being the most (least) number of remaining resources (requests) of a job, the system must have at least _____ resources.

E9   Deadlock (prevention / avoidance) _____ is not practical.

E10   Deadlock recovery always requires identifying a _____ process/job to be terminated.

E11   The situation when every process in a set is waiting for an event that can only be caused by another process in the set is called _____

E12   The condition where at least one resource is held in a non-sharable mode is called _____

E13   The condition where a process is holding one resource and waiting to acquire additional resources is called

_____

E14   The condition where a resource can be released only voluntarily by the process holding the resource is called

_____

E15   A simple mechanism of deadlock recovery is

_____

E16   Deadlock state is a subset of _____ state.

E17   The minimum number of processes required for a deadlock to occur is _____

E18   In a resource-allocation graph, a directed edge from a process to a resource is called a _____

E19   In a resource-allocation graph, a directed edge from a resource to a process is called an _____

E20   In a resource-allocation graph, a directed edge indicating that a process may request a resource at some time in the future is called

_____

E21   A situation where the system can allocate resources to each process in some order, and still avoid a deadlock is called

_____

E22   Presence of a cycle in the _____ graph indicates deadlock.

E23   Presence of a cycle in the _____ graph may not indicate deadlock.

E24   In a system with 15 instances of some resource, and each process requiring 3 instances of the resource, the maximum number of processes for which the system never enters into deadlock is ___

E25   In a system with 3 processes sharing resources of the same type, with peak demands of 3, 4 and 6, the minimum number of resources of that type required to ensure that a deadlock will not occur is ___

E26   With three resources, R_1, R_2, and R_3, each assigned unique integer values 12, 10, and 15, respectively, the resource ordering which prevents a circular wait is _____

E27   With three resources, R_1, R_2, and R_3, each assigned unique integer values 18, 20, and 14, respectively, the resource ordering which prevents a circular wait is _____

E28   At some point of time, if L is the minimum of the remaining resources required across all jobs, and A is the available resources in the system, the condition that should hold for the system to be in *safe state* is _____

E29   The graph derived from the resource allocation graph by removing the resource nodes and collapsing the appropriate edges is called

_____

E30   Mechanisms for deadlock handling are provided by the

_____

E31   The four conditions that must hold simultaneously in a system for a deadlock to occur are _____,
_____,   _____,   and

_____

E32   In a system with one resource type, and 3 user processes whose maximum demands for the resource are 3, 4, and 5, the *minimum* instances of the resource required to ensure that deadlock will never occur, is _____

E33   In a system with 3 user processes, each requiring 2 units of resource R, the *minimum* number of units (instances) of R such that no deadlocks will ever arise is _____

E34   Given that the instances of a resource needed by processes P_1, P_2, ... P_N are R_1, R_2, ... R_N, respectively, the minimum number of resource instances required to ensure that deadlock will never occur is _____

E35   The minimum number of resources (of the same type) which are shared by 3 processes which have peak demands of X, Y, and Z instances   of   the   resource   is

_____

E36   Given N processes and each process needing a maximum of M resources (of the same type), the *minimum* number of resources, R to ensure that the system is deadlock free, is

_____

E37   The condition that always holds (invariant) between the sum of the elements of a column j of the *allocation matrix C*, the jth elements of the *existence vector E*, and the *available vector A*, is

_____

E38   Given that C_K is the sum of the values of the Kth column of the current allocation matrix, the relationship between the Kth elements of existence vector E, the Kth element of available vector A, and C_K is _____

E39   Given that there are N nodes in the resource graph, and the time taken (on the average) to detect a cycle is T, the *best case* time for detecting a deadlock is _____ (Cycle detected by the cycle detection algorithm on the first node chosen)

E40   Given that there are N nodes in the resource graph, and the time taken (on the average) to detect a cycle is T, the *worst case* time for detecting a deadlock is _____ (Cycle is detected when processing the last node or cycle is not detected)

E41   In a system with 12 instances of a resource and 3 processes, and given the maximum resource needs of 5, 8, 7, and current allocations of 3, 5, 4, respectively, the system is in _____ state.

E42   In a system with 12 instances of a resource and 3 processes, and given the maximum resource needs of 10, 3, 7, and current allocations of 4, 2, 4, respectively, the system is in _____ state.

E43   In a system with 12 instances of a resource and 3 processes, and given the maximum resource needs of 6, 4, 7, and current allocations of 5, 2, 4, respectively, the system is in _____ state.

E44   In a system with 10 instances of a resource and 3 processes, and given the maximum resource needs of 10, 5, 8, and current allocations of 4, 4, 1, respectively, the system is in _____ state.

E45　In a system with 14 instances of a resource and 4 processes, and given the maximum resource needs of 5, 8, 7, 3, and current allocations of 3, 5, 4, 1, respectively, the system is in _____ state.

E46　In a system with 14 instances of a resource and 4 processes, and given the maximum resource needs of 4, 6, 5, 9, and current allocations of 1, 4, 0, 8, respectively, the system is in _____ state.

E47　In a system with 10 instances of a resource and 3 processes, and given the maximum resource needs of 10, 3, 6, and current allocations of 4, 1, 4, respectively, the system is in _____ state.

E48　In a system with 10 instances of a resource and 3 processes, and given the maximum resource needs of 10, 3, 6, and current allocations of 6, 2, 1, respectively, the system is in _____ state.

E49　In a system with 12 instances of a resource and 3 processes, and given the maximum resource needs of 10, 4, 7, and current allocations of 4, 2, 4, respectively, the system is in _____ state.

E50　In a system with 10 instances of a resource and 3 processes, and given the maximum resource needs of 8, 2, 6, and a set of current allocations which would result in the system being in *unsafe* state is _____

E51　In a system with 12 instances of a resource and 3 processes, and given the maximum resource needs of 12, 4, 7, and a set of current allocations which would result in the system being in *unsafe* state is _____

E52　Given a system with ({allocated}; {waiting-for}) tuples for three process to be P1: (R2; None), P2: (R1; R3), and P3: (R3; R2), the system is (deadlocked / not deadlocked) _____

E53　Given a system with ({allocated}; {waiting-for}) tuples for three process to be P1: (R2; R1), P2: (R1; R3), and P3: (R3; R2), the system is (deadlocked / not deadlocked) _____

E54 Given a system with ({allocated}; {waiting-for}) tuples for three process to be P1: (R1; R3), P2: (R3; R1), and P3: (R2; None), the system is (deadlocked / not deadlocked) _____ (P1 is holding R1 which P2 needs, and P2 is holding R3 which P1 needs)

E55 Given a system with ({allocated}; {waiting-for}) tuples for three process to be P1: (R2; None), P2: (R3; R1), and P3: (R1; R2), the system is (deadlocked / not deadlocked)

_____

E56 Given a system with ({allocated}; {waiting-for}) tuples for three process to be P1: (R3; None), P2: (R2; R1), and P3: (R1; R2), the system is (deadlocked / not deadlocked)

_____

E57 Given a system with ({allocated}; {waiting-for}) tuples for three process to be P1: (R2, R3; None), P2: (None; R1), and P3: (R1; R2), the system is (deadlocked / not deadlocked)

_____

E58 Given a system consisting of M resources of the same type shared by N processes, with resources requested and released by processes only one at a time, for the system to be deadlock free, the maximum need of each process is between _____ and _____ resources.

E59 Given a system consisting of M resources of the same type shared by N processes, with resources requested and released by processes only one at a time, for the system to be deadlock free, the sum of all maximum needs is less than _____

E60 The difference of the vectors E (resources in existence) and A (resources available) represents

_____

E61 In the *banker's* algorithm the vector of length M, where M is the number of resource types, denotes the _____ of the resources.

E62 In a system with N processes and M resource types, the _____ matrix in the *banker's* algorithm denotes the resources allocated to processes.

E63 In a system with *N* processes and *M* resource types, the *max* matrix in the *banker's* algorithm denotes the _____ of the processes.

E64 In a system with N processes and M resource types, the *need* matrix in the *banker's* algorithm is obtained by subtracting the _____ matrix from the _____ matrix.

E65 In a system with N instances of a single resource, out of which M (< N) of the resource instances have been allocated, the condition to be satisfied by the resource need Q of any process P_i such that the system will be in a safe state, is _____

E66 Given 12 processes sharing 17 instances of a resource, which are reserved and released one at a time, and a sufficient condition for T_R, the sum of the maximum resource needs of all processes to ensure no deadlock, is _____

E67 Given a system with resource types, R1 and R2, each with two instances, and 4 processes with corresponding ({requested}; {allocated}) tuples to be P1: (R1; R2), P2: (− ; R1), P3: (R2; R1), P4: (− ; R2), the resource allocation graph (does/does not) _____ have a cycle, and (is / is not) _____ deadlocked.

E68 Given a system with resource types R1 and R2, each with two instances, and 4 processes with corresponding ({requested}; {allocated}) tuples to be P1: (R1; R2), P2: (R2 ; R1), P3: (R2; R1), P4: (− ; R2), the resource allocation graph (does/does not) _____ have a cycle, and (is / is not) _____ deadlocked.

E69 Given a system with two types of resources, R1 and R2, each with two instances, and four processes with corresponding ({requested}; {allocated}) tuples to be P1: (R1; R2), P2: (R2; R1), P3: (R2; R1), P4: (R1 ; R2), the resource allocation graph (does/does not) _____ have a cycle, and (is / is not) _____ deadlocked.

E70   Given a system with three types of resources, R1, R2, and R3, with one, two, and one instances, respectively, and three processes with corresponding ({requested}; {allocated}) tuples to be P1: (R1; R2), P2: (R3; {R1, R2}), P3: (R2; R3), the resource allocation graph (does/does not) _____ have a cycle, and (is / is not) _____ deadlocked.

E71   Given a system has 12 instances of a resource, and 3 processes with their respective (*maximum need, currently owned*) tuples to be (10, 4), (3, 2), and (7, 4), the state of the system is in _____ state.

F. Memory management and virtual memory

F1 The hardware unit that maps logical (virtual) addresses to physical addresses is the _____

F2 The _____ in the page table indicates whether the page is in a physical frame or not.

F3 A reference to a page that is not in main memory results in _____

F4 The _____ is indexed by the physical frame number and the entries are page numbers.

F5 The number of entries in the TLB multiplied by the page size is the _____

F6 The page table entry contains the _____

F7 The contents of the entries in a TLB are _____ and _____

F8 The contents of the entries in segment table are _____ and _____

F9 The _____ bit is useful when a page is selected for replacement.

F10 The _____ contains the starting address of the page table in memory.

F11 In a TLB, all the entries are searched simultaneously using _____ technology.

F12 A page fault causes a _____ to the operating system.

F13 When the CPU generates a logical address (for instruction or data), its corresponding page number is first looked up in the _____

F14 The addresses generated by the CPU are _____ addresses.

F15   The addresses generated by the memory management unit (MMU) are _____ addresses.

F16   In a *hashed* page table, the entries are the hash values of
_____

F17   Paging has _____ fragmentation.

F18   _____ has external fragmentation.

F19   A running process requesting more memory (dynamically) may not result in relocation of the entire process under _____ (memory allocation).

F20   Translation of virtual addresses to physical addresses under segmentation requires _____ register and _____ register.

F21   By paging the segments, wasted memory due to _____ is reduced.

F22   When a program occupies only a small portion of its large virtual address space, the preferred address mapping is the use of
_____

F23   Contiguous memory allocation scheme suffers from _____ fragmentation.

F24   Pure segmentation scheme suffers from _____ fragmentation.

F25   Paging suffers from _____ fragmentation.

F26   The actual starting address of a job/process in main memory is stored in the _____ register.

F27   For each active job, the size of the job and the memory location where the page table is stored is in the _____

F28   In a page size of 512 bytes, the *maximum* possible unused bytes is
_____

F29   In a page size of 2048 bytes, the *minimum* possible unused bytes is _____

F30   In a system with N processes, the number of page tables (page map tables) is _____

F31   Given that a process of N pages accesses K ($\leq N$) distinct pages during its execution, the minimum number of page faults is

_____

F32   The main memory frame numbers corresponding to the logical page numbers of a process is contained in the

_____

F33   A page selected for swapping out is not written on disk if the _____ bit is not set.

F34   With increase of cache access time, the average memory access time _____

F35   With increase in TLB size, the average memory access time

_____

F36   The entries of a translation look-aside buffer (TLB) are implemented as _____

F37   Each entry in an Inverted Page Table contains a pair _____ and _____

F38   The page needed at the farthest point in the future is the candidate for replacement in the _____ page replacement algorithm.

F39   The page referenced at the farthest point in the past is the candidate for replacement in the _____ page replacement algorithm.

F40   The set of pages used by some number of most recent memory references is called _____

F41   The _____ is an approximation of a program's locality.

F42   Only a fraction of a process's _____ needs to be stored in the TLB.

F43   Cache works on the principle of _____

F44   The single cache where instructions and data stored is called

_____

F45   A currently referenced memory location being highly likely to be
        referenced   again   in   the   near   future   is   called

_____

F46   Accessing a given set of memory locations repetitively over a
        short period of time is called _____

F47   The high likelihood of references to memory locations in the near
        future which are closer to currently referenced locations is called

_____

F48   Accessing a given set of memory locations repetitively, which are
        in close physical proximity (memory addresses) is called

_____

F49   The *minimum* internal fragmentation in a system with a page size
        of P bytes, is _____

F50   The *maximum* internal fragmentation in a system with a page
        size of P bytes, is _____

F51   An address generated by a CPU is referred to as

_____

F52   The mapping of a logical address to a physical address is done in
        hardware by the _____

F53   With   segmentation,   a   logical   address   consists   of
        _____ and _____

F54   The starting address of the page table in memory is contained in
        the _____

F55   There is a *valid-invalid* bit for every _____

F56   The separation of physical memory and logical memory is
        provided by the concept of _____

F57   A cache _____ refers to the case when a CPU reference
        cannot be found in cache.

F58 The simplest mapping technique which maps each block of main memory into only one possible cache line is called

_____

F59 The _____ bits are used to determine which memory block is resident in a cache line.

F60 The mapping where any main memory block can be mapped to any cache line is called _____

F61 The technique (mode) where all write operations made to main memory are immediately made to the cache as well is called

_____

F62 The technique (mode) where all write operations made to main memory are written to the cache at a later time is called

_____

F63 The _____ cache design eliminates contention for the cache between the instruction fetch/decode unit and the execution unit.

F64 Wasted space within a partition is called _____

F65 Page numbers are given by _____ order bits of the logical address.

F66 Offsets within a page are given by _____ order bits of the logical address.

F67 Variable size segments are further divided into fixed size pages in the _____ scheme.

F68 During page replacement, selection of the victim from among the pages of the same process is called _____

F69 During page replacement, selection of the victim page from among the pages of any process is called _____

F70 On a TLB miss, the operating system accesses the

_____

F71 In _____ paging, a page is brought into memory only when it is accessed / needed.

F72   The byte offset in memory frame with respect to the byte offset in the corresponding page is (larger / the same / smaller) _____

F73   The mapping information of logical pages to main memory frames is contained in _____

F74   The _____ field in the page table indicates whether the page is in a memory frame or not.

F75   The *reference* field of the page table is used by _____

F76   The _____ field of the page table is used to decide if a page is selected for replacement should be written on disk.

F77   The leftover space when a process gets more memory than its requirement, is called _____

F78   The condition when a referenced page number is not present in the TLB is called _____

F79   Every reference to a data (in the worst case) has two memory accesses – one access for _____, and the other for _____

F80   The hash values in the entries of a hashed page table correspond to _____

F81   The maximum logical address that the CPU is allowed to access is contained in the _____ register.

F82   The dynamic storage-allocation algorithm which results in the smallest leftover hole in memory is _____

F83   The dynamic storage-allocation algorithm which results in the largest leftover hole in memory is _____

F84   A(n) _____ page table has one page entry for each frame of memory (RAM).

F85   With a page size of 8 KB, the number of bits required to represent the byte offset in the logical address is _____

F86 The number of entries in the page table where 18 bits of a logical address represent an entry in the page table, is _____

F87 With segmentation, a logical address consists of _____ and _____

F88 The location of segment table in memory is in _____

F89 The number of segments used by a program is in _____

F90 The condition when a process spends more time paging than executing is called _____

F91 Swapping out is the processes of moving a page from _____ to _____

F92 The situation where there is enough total memory space, but the available space is not contiguous to satisfy a request, is called _____

F93 A segment is spread across several pages in the _____ memory management system.

F94 Use of combinations of main memory (RAM) and disk storage to provide each process a view of a large contiguous space is called _____

F95 Recent translations of virtual memory to physical memory are stored in _____

F96 Bringing pages into memory frames (based on prediction) even before they are accessed is called _____

F97 The _____ bit is useful in making page replacement efficient.

F98 The page number corresponds to the _____ order bits of the logical address.

F99 The _____ bits in a page table entry indicate the kinds of permissible operations on the page.

F100 The inverted page table is _____ than the (normal) page table.

F101 The contents of the entries in segment table are _____ and _____

F102 The _____ bit is useful when a page is selected for replacement.

F103 The _____ algorithm, although not implementable, is used for assessing performance of other page-replacement schemes.

F104 The table in main memory which contains segment information, including the segment number and its corresponding memory address, is called _____

F105 A _____ scheme requires that the entire program be stored contiguously.

F106 In a _____ scheme programs may be relocated to different parts of memory.

F107 The highest location in memory accessible by a program is stored in _____

F108 The starting address of a process in memory is stored in the _____

F109 Loading only a part of the program into memory as required is called _____

F110 Using the page that has been in memory the longest as candidate for removal is used in _____ page replacement algorithm.

F111 The page replacement algorithm that is often used in practice is the _____

F112 The four factors in the design of cache memory are _____, _____, _____, and _____

F113   The two major cache rewrite policies are _____
        and _____

F114   A memory allocation scheme in which jobs are given as
        much memory as they request when they are loaded for
        processing, is called _____

F115   _____ are used as indices to look up the page table to get
        corresponding physical frames.

F116   In a 2 level paging system with 10 bits each for page address and
        12 bits for the offset, the page size is _____

F117   In a 2 level paging system with 32-bit virtual address, first-level
        page address of 10 bits, and a page size of 4KB, the number of
        page tables at level 1 is _____

F118   In a 2 level paging system with 32-bit virtual address, 12 bits for
        first-level page address, and a page size of 1KB, the number of
        page tables at level 2 is _____

F119   The mechanism which enables execution of programs larger than
        can fit in memory (RAM) is called _____

F120   Physical memory is divided into equal sized units called
        _____

F121   Virtual memory is divided into equal sized units called
        _____

F122   The bit in the page table entry used to indicate whether the page
        is valid (i.e. currently in memory) or not is called
        _____

F123   The problem of a large and sparse page table resulting from a large
        virtual address space is solved by having a(n)
        _____

F124   A TLB with added process identifiers to the TLB lines is called
        _____

F125   A _____ swaps a page into memory only if that
        page is needed.

F126 An *offset* in the logical address which is greater than the *limit* field of the segment table entry generates a _____

F127 Increasing the number of page frames in main memory could resulting in increased page faults under FIFO page replacement is referred to as _____ anomaly.

F128 The worst case number of page faults that can occur in the execution of an instruction which reads two variables, does an operation on them, and writes the result to another variable, is ____ (one each for instruction read, two data reads, and one data write).

F129 When a program uses only a small portion of its virtual address space a _____ page table is preferred.

F130 Under-allocation of the minimum number of pages required by a process causes _____

F131 A very low CPU utilization and a high disk usage is indicative of _____

F132 A string of referenced page numbers is called _____

F133 The number of entries in a conventional page table in a system with 32-bit logical address and a page size of 4 KB, is _____

F134 Given a system with *M* memory frames (initially empty) and a reference string of length *R* containing *P* (> *M*) distinct page numbers, the *minimum* possible number of page faults is _____

F135 Given a system with *M* memory frames (initially empty) and a reference string of length *R*, the *maximum* possible number of page faults is _____

F136 Given a system with *M* memory frames (initially empty) and a reference string of length *R*, the *minimum* number of distinct page numbers in the reference string which results in the *maximum* possible number of page faults is _____

F137   The effective memory access time in a system with a TLB hit ratio of h%, TLB access time of t_1 units, and main memory access time of t_2 units, is _____

F138   Given a system with a cache access time of 3 nS, main memory access time of 75 nS, in order to have the effective memory access time to be less than 9 nS, the least cache hit ratio required is _____

F139   Given a system with a cache with access time of 5 nS and a hit ratio of 0.95, to achieve effective memory access time to be no more than 10 nS, the required main memory access time should be at most _____

F140   The optimum page size in a system with average process size of S bytes and each page table entry of E bytes, is _____

F141   The average page access time in a system with a page hit ratio of 0.7, main memory access time of a page of 10 ns and secondary memory access time of a page of 1 millisecond, is _____

F142   The number of pages in a system with page size of 8 KB and a 48-bit virtual address, is _____

F143   Of the two memory (RAM) accesses required for any instruction or data access, one is for _____ (to get the frame number), and the other for the _____

F144   The minimum possible number of pages of a process of N pages that could be resident in main memory (at any point) during the execution of the process is _____

F145   The maximum possible number of pages of a process of N pages that could be resident in main memory (at any point) during the execution of the process is _____

F146   The minimum possible number of pages of a process of N pages that are brought into main memory (at some point) before the process finishes execution of is _____

F147   The minimum possible number of pages of a process of N pages that could have been swapped out (at any point) during its execution is _____

F148   In a byte addressable system with V bits of virtual (logical) address, a page size of P bytes, and M pages of a process in memory, the number of entries with valid bits not set in the page table is _____

F149   Given a byte addressable system with V bits of virtual address, a page size of P bytes, and a process with a total of N pages, out of which M are in memory, the number of entries with valid bits set in the page table is _____

F150   Given a physical memory of M frames (initially all empty) and the page-reference string of length P, with N (> M) *distinct* page numbers occurring in it, the minimum number of page faults is _____

F151   Given a physical memory of M frames (initially all empty) and the page-reference string of length P (> M), the maximum possible number of page faults is _____

F152   In a demand-page system with probability of a page fault of p, memory access time of t, and page-fault handling time of f, the effective access time is _____

F153   In a system with M bytes of virtual address space, page size of K bytes, and each page table entry of P bytes, the size of the page table, is _____

F154   In a system with N bits in the page table entry to hold the frame number, and page size of K bytes, the physical memory (RAM) size is _____

F155   In a system with a TLB hit ratio of 90%, TLB access time of 20 nS, and main memory access time of 100 nS, the effective memory access time is _____

F156   In a system with a TLB hit ratio of 95%, TLB access time of 10 nS, and main memory access time of 120 nS, the effective memory access time is _____

F157   In a system with a TLB hit ratio of 90%, TLB access time of 15 nS, and main memory access time of 85 nS, the effective memory access time is _____

F158   In a system with TLB access time of 15 nS and main memory access time of 100 nS, the TLB hit ratio required to achieve an effective memory access time of 120 nS, is _____

F159   In a system with main memory access time of 250 nS and a cache hit ratio of 95%, the cache access time required to have average memory access time of 32.5 nS, is _____

F160   In a system with 32-bit virtual addresses, page size of 4 KB, a 4-way set associative translation look-aside buffer (TLB) of 128 entries, the number of bits in the TLB tag is _____

F161   In a system with 32-bit virtual addresses, page size of 4 KB, a 4-way set associative translation look-aside buffer (TLB) of 64 entries, the number of bits in the TLB tag is _____

F162   Given the logical address 0xAB76 (in hexadecimal) with a page size of 256 bytes, the page number is _____

F163   Given the logical address 0xAE9C (in hexadecimal) with a page size of 256 bytes, the offset within the page is _____

F164   Given the logical address 0xAB76 (in hexadecimal) with a page size of 1024 bytes, the page number is _____

F165   Given the logical address 0xAB76 (in hexadecimal) with a page size of 1024 bytes, the offset within the page is _____

F166   Given the logical address 0xAE9C (in hexadecimal) with a page size of 1024 bytes, the page number is _____

F167   Given the logical address 0xAE9C (in hexadecimal) with a page size of 1024 bytes, the offset within the page is _____

F168   In a two-level paging system with an 8 KB page size, and a 32-bit logical address, and the outer page table with 1024 entries, the number of bits are used to represent the second-level page table is

_____

F169   In a system with average main memory (RAM) access time of 250 nS, and average cache access time of 30 nS, the *cache hit ratio* required to have an average memory access time of at least 50 nS, is _____

F170   A(n) _____ matches the process with each entry in the TLB.

F171   The _____ register is used to check for invalid memory addresses generated by a CPU.

F172   The *minimum* possible number of page faults for a process with 10 pages, and 4 main memory frames, with all the pages being accessed during the execution of the process, is _____

F173   The *maximum* possible number of page faults for a process with 10 pages, and 4 main memory frames, and 17 references to pages during the execution of the process, is _____

F174   In a system with 3 main memory frames, and a process referencing pages in the order: *A, C, C, B, A, D, F, E, F, F, G, F, D, A, B*, the *hit ratio* using *FIFO* page replacement algorithm is _____

F175   In a system with 3 main memory frames, and a process referencing pages in the order: *A, C, C, B, A, D, F, E, F, F, G, F, D, A, B*, the final content of the frames using *FIFO* page replacement algorithm is _____

F176   In a system with 3 main memory frames, and a process referencing pages in the order: *A, C, C, B, A, D, F, E, F, F, G, F, D, A, B*, the *hit ratio* using *LRU* page replacement algorithm is _____

F177   In a system with 3 main memory frames, and a process referencing pages in the order: *A, C, C, B, A, D, F, E, F, F, G, F, D, A, B*, the final content of the frames using *LRU* page replacement algorithm is _____

F178   In a system with 3 main memory frames, and a process referencing pages in the order: *A, C, C, B, A, D, F, E, F, F, G, F, D, A, B*, the *hit ratio* using *OPT* page replacement algorithm is _____

F179   In a system with 3 main memory frames, and a process referencing pages in the order: *A, C, A, B, B, E, A, F, B*, the *hit ratio* using *FIFO* page replacement algorithm is _____

F180   In a system with 3 main memory frames, and a process referencing pages in the order: *A, C, A, B, B, E, A, F, B*, the final content of the frames using *FIFO* page replacement algorithm is _____

F181   In a system with 3 main memory frames, and a process referencing pages in the order: *A, C, A, B, B, E, A, F, B,* the *hit ratio* using *LRU* page replacement algorithm is _____

F182   In a system with 3 main memory frames, and a process referencing pages in the order: *A, C, A, B, B, E, A, F, B,* the final content of the frames using *LRU* page replacement algorithm is _____

F183   In a system with 3 main memory frames, and a process referencing pages in the order: *A, C, A, B, B, E, A, F, B,* the *hit ratio* using *OPT* page replacement algorithm is _____

F184   The size of a process which requires four 256-byte pages with a fragmentation of 55 bytes, is _____

F185   The fragmentation of a process with a size of 1500 Bytes if the page size is 256 bytes, is _____

F186   The size of a process which uses six 256–byte pages and has the minimum fragmentation, is _____

F187   The size of a process which uses four 256–byte pages and has the maximum fragmentation, is _____

F188   In a system with a page size of 256 bytes, the number of pages required for a process of 2000 bytes, is _____

F189   In a system with a page size of 256 bytes, the page number where an item with byte address 925 be located, is _____

F190   In a system with a page size of 256 bytes, the size of a program which requires 4 pages and has a fragmentation of 45 bytes, is

_____

F191   In a system with a page size of 256 bytes, the fragmentation of a process with a size of 1600 bytes is _____

F192   In a system with a page size of 256 bytes, the displacement (offset) of an item with a byte address of 342 is _____

F193   In a paged memory system with a page size of 512 bytes, the number of pages required for a process of size 4,000 bytes, is

_____

F194   In a system with a page size of 512 bytes, the fragmentation (unused bytes) for a process of size 4,000 bytes, is

_____

F195   In a system with a page size of 512 bytes, for a process of size 4,000 bytes, the page which holds an item located at byte number 2020 of the process (page 0 being the first page), is

_____

F196   In a paged memory system with a page size of 512 bytes, the size of a process which takes up 5 pages and leaves unused space of 300 bytes, is _____

F197   In a paged memory system with a page size of 512 bytes, the page that holds an item located at byte number 800 of a process, (page 0 being the first page), is _____

F198   If a system can allocate all resources requested by all processes (up to their stated maximums) without entering a deadlock state, it is said to be in _____

F199   In a K-level hierarchy of paging, the number of memory accesses (in the worst case) to access a data item is _____

F200   The number of bits in the memory address for a main memory size of 4GB is _____

F201   The number of frames in a main memory size of 4GB with a frame size of 2KB is _____

F202   In a system with 32-bit virtual address and main memory frame size of 2 KB, the number of page table entries is

_____

F203   In a system with 20-bit physical address, and a frame size of 1 KB, the number of main memory frames is _____

F204   Given a logical address space of 4GB, a page table with 2M entries, and a physical memory of 256 MB, the number of bits in logical address is _____

F205   Given a logical address space of 4GB, a page table with 2M entries, and a physical memory of 256 MB, the number of bits in physical address is _____

F206 Given a logical address space of 4GB, a page table with 2M entries, and a physical memory of 256 MB, the number of bits of address required to index a page is ____, and to index a frame is _____

F207 Given that logical address consists of 16 bits and the page size is 512 bytes, the number of pages is _____

F208 In a system with a logical address of 20 bits and 2K pages, the page size is _____

F209 In a system with a physical memory of 256 frames, each of size 1024 bytes, the number of bits in the physical address is _____

F210 Given that a page table entry has 15 bits for frame number, and a main memory frame size is 2048 bytes the size of main memory is _____

F211 In a system with a physical memory frame size of 4KB and 4096 *entries* in the page table, the number of bits of logical address is _____

F212 In a system with a 128MB virtual address space and a physical memory frame size of 2KB, the number of *entries* in the page table is _____

F213 In a system with a page size of 2 KB, the number of bits in the logical address required to denote the offset within a page is _____

F214 Given that a logical address consists of 16 bits and the page size is 512 bytes, the number of pages is _____

F215 In a (byte addressable) system with a logical address of 20 bits and 4096 pages, the page size is _____

F216 Given that a system has 8K pages and each page is 2K bytes, the number of bits in the logical address is _____

F217 Given that the physical memory has 256 frames, each of size 1024 bytes, the bits in the physical address is _____

F218   Given that a page table has 1024 entries and each entry has 9 bits for a frame number, the number of frames of physical memory is

_____

F219   In a (byte addressable) system with a logical address of 20 bits and 2048 pages, the page size is _____

F220   In a system with 2048 pages, the number of bits for byte offset within a page of 9 bits, the size of logical address space is

_____

F221   In a system with 2048 pages, main memory of 256 frames, the size of the page table assuming 4 status bits, is

_____

F222   In a system with a physical memory of 256 frames, each of size 512 bytes, the number of bits in the physical address is _____

F223   Given that the logical address is 32 bits, and the page size is 4096 bytes, the number of pages is _____

F224   Given that the page size is 4096 bytes and 256 frames in the main memory, the number of bits in the physical address is

_____

F225   Given that a system has virtual memory space of 2^{32} bytes, and page size is 4096 bytes, the number of page table entries is

_____

F226   Given a page size of 4 KB, the number of bits required for the page offset in the logical address is _____

F227   In a (byte addressable) system with a 24 bits logical address and 4096 pages, the page size is _____

F228   In a system with 2048 pages and each page of size 512 bytes, the number of bits in logical address is _____

F229   In a system with a logical address space of 4GB, and a page size of 4KB, the number of bits for indexing a page is _____

F230   In a system with a physical memory of 4K frames, each of size 1K bytes, the number of bits in the physical address is _____

F231   In a 64-bit machine, with 2 GB RAM, and 8 KB page size, the number of entries in the inverted page table is _____

F232   In a system with a page size of 512 bytes, each page table entry having 11 bits for the frame number, the physical memory size is

_____

F233   For a process with N pages, the number of entries in the page table is _____

F234   For a process with N pages, each page of P bytes, the size of the process is _____

F235   In a system with N bits of physical address, and a page size of P bytes, the number of entries in the inverted page table is _____

F236   Given a virtual address of 32 bits and a page size of 4KB, the number of bits in the address for the page number is _____

F237   Given a virtual address of 32 bits and, the number of bits in the physical address for offset within a frame of 11 bits, the number of pages is _____

F238   Given a virtual address of 32 bits and 22 bits in the physical address for the page number, the page size is _____

F239   Given a system with a main memory size of 4GB, cache size of 1 MB, and a cache line size of 64 bytes, the number of cache lines, is _____

F240   Given a system with a main memory size of 4GB, cache size of 1 MB, and a cache line size of 64 bytes, the possible number of memory blocks that would map to a given cache line using direct mapping, is _____

F241   Given a system with a main memory size of 4GB, cache size of 1 MB, and a cache line size of 64 bytes, the size of the cache tag, assuming a fully associative mapping, is _____

F242   Given a system with a main memory size of 4GB, cache size of 1 MB, and a cache line size of 64 bytes, the size of the cache tag, assuming a 4-way associative mapping, the number of bits for addressing a set is _____

F243   Given a system with a main memory size of 4GB, cache size of 1 MB, and a cache line size of 64 bytes, the size of the cache tag, assuming a 4-way associative mapping, the number of tag bits is _____

F244   In a paged memory system with a page size of 512 bytes, the size of a process requiring 5 pages, and having a fragmentation of 200 bytes, is _____

F245   Given five memory partitions M_1 to M_5 of 100 KB, 450 KB, 250 KB, 300 KB, and 500 KB, and four processes P_1 to P_4 with memory requirements of 210 KB, 325 KB, 127 KB, and 432 KB, the assignment of processes to partitions using *first-fit* allocation is _____

F246   Given five memory partitions M_1 to M_5 of 100 KB, 450 KB, 250 KB, 300 KB, and 500 KB, and four processes P_1 to P_4 with memory requirements of 210 KB, 325 KB, 127 KB, and 432 KB, the assignment of processes to partitions using *best-fit* allocation is _____

F247   Given five memory partitions M_1 to M_5 of 100 KB, 450 KB, 250 KB, 300 KB, and 500 KB, and four processes P_1 to P_4 with memory requirements of 210 KB, 325 KB, 127 KB, and 432 KB, the assignment of processes to partitions using *worst-fit* allocation is _____

F248   Given a system with a 1 KB page size, and the address 2563 (given as decimal numbers), the corresponding page number is _____ and the offset is _____

F249   Given a system with a 1 KB page size, and the address 18967 (given as decimal numbers), the corresponding page number is _____ and the offset is _____

F250   Given a logical address space of 64 pages and 1024 bytes per page, mapped onto a physical memory of 16 frames, the number of bits required in the logical address is _____ and the number of bits required in the physical address is _____

F251   The fields in each node of the linked list in each entry of the hashed page table are _____, _____, and _____

F252   The effective instruction time in a system with (average) instruction execution time of I units, (average) page fault handling time of J units, and average page fault rate of one every K instructions, is _____

F253   The context switch overhead time for swapping out a 50 MB process and bringing in a 25 MB process, with a disk transfer rate of 50 MB per second, and average disk latency of 4 milliseconds, is _____

F254   Given F is the page fault rate (%), H is the page hit rate (%), T is the time to service a page fault, and M is the memory access time, the *average memory access time* is _____

F255   Given that a system has two cache options: (a) with access time of 3 ns and a hit ratio of 0.96, and (b) with access time of 3.5ns and a hit ratio of 0.97, the upper bound on the memory access time when option (b) is beneficial, is _____

F256   The (byte addressable) logical address space corresponding to V bits of logical address is _____

F257   In a system with V bits of logical address and a page size of 2^K bytes, the number of bits in the logical address used for the page number is _____

F258   In a system with V bits of logical address and 2^P pages, the number of bits in the logical address used for indexing a byte within a page is _____

F259   In a system with logical address space of 2^V bytes and K lower order bits in the logical address used for byte offset within a page, the number of pages is _____

F260   In a (byte addressable) system with V bits of logical address out of which P bits are for page number, the page size is _____

F261   In a (byte addressable) system with V bits of logical address and K bits for a byte offset within a page, the number of pages is _____

F262   In a system with a virtual address space of 2^V bytes and page size of 2^K bytes, the number of logical pages of a process is _____

F263 In a system with physical address space of 2^P bytes and page size of 2^K bytes, the number of physical frames in the system is

_____

F264 In a system with K bits for a byte offset within a page, and 2^E bytes per page table entry, the number of page table entries is

_____

F265 In a system using hierarchical paging with a virtual address space of 2^V bytes, page size of 2^K bytes, and 2^E bytes per page table entry, the number of pages required to store the innermost page table entries, is _____

F266 In a system using hierarchical paging with $L \, (\geq 2)$ levels, a virtual address space of 2^V bytes, page size of 2^K bytes, and 2^E bytes per page table entry, L (in terms of V, K, and E) is given by

_____

F267 In a system using hierarchical paging with $L \, (\geq 2)$ levels, a virtual address space of 2^V bytes, page size of 2^K bytes, and 2^E bytes per page table entry, V_0 – the number of (most significant) bits of the virtual address that are used as an index into the outermost page table – is given by _____

G. I/O subsystem

G1   _____ contains the list of processes waiting for a particular I/O device.

G2   The mechanism which facilitates the sharing of a printer (but not at the same time) among different processes is called _____

G3   The _____ processes I/O interrupts and handles error conditions.

G4   Code / software to control I/O devices are in _____

G5   The registers of the I/O devices are mapped into the memory space of the processor in _____

G6   The processor has special I/O instructions to control the IO device directly in _____

G7   When I/O is slow or of large sizes, _____ is more efficient.

G8   Interrupt driven I/O is more efficient than polling for _____ I/O devices.

G9   The _____ acts as the interface between the CPU and the peripheral devices.

G10   There is a single address space for memory locations and I/O devices in _____ I/O.

G11   In _____ mode the I/O module and main memory exchange data directly, without processor involvement.

G12   The processor need not wait for the duration of I/O, but continue with the execution of program instructions in the _____ mode of I/O.

G13   The CPU waiting for the I/O operation to complete, by repeatedly checking the device status is called _____

G14   In _____, the CPU must periodically scan (read) an address to check if an input has arrived.

G15   The CPU accesses the device memory much like it accesses main memory in _____ I/O.

G16   The inability of the CPU to do a memory access when the DMA controller is doing data transfer is called _____

G17   The *device-dependent* software for a device (or class of devices) is contained in _____

G18   The hardware that controls (operates) the actual device is called

_____

G19   There is no explicit I/O instruction in a CPU with _____ I/O.

G20   When I/O completion times are known to be long, _____ are better suited for handling I/O.

G21   The error detection in I/O operations is the responsibility of the

_____

G22   A(n) _____ is the interface between the CPU and the peripheral device.

G23   For CPUs having memory-mapped I/O, protection of I/O is ensured by _____

G24   In _____ the CPU is tied up during a data transfer from the device to I/O module.

G25   When the I/O is frequent and of short duration, _____ is a better I/O mechanism.

G26   The three major modes of I/O are _____, _____, and _____

G27   The *device driver* provides an interface between the _____ and the _____

G28   The device controller communicates with the operating system via the _____

G29   The hardware which operates the device is called the

_____

G30   In DMA the interrupt signaling I/O completion is sent to the CPU by the _____

G31   The module of the operating system responsible for controlling the use of devices is the _____

G32   If the processor iterates a busy-waiting loop many times before the I/O completes, use of _____ is better than

_____

G33   An I/O which does not put a process in a waiting state is called _____ I/O.

G34   In a system with a device generating 800 interrupts per second, and each interrupt processing consuming 100 μs, the fraction of processor time consumed for interrupt processing is _____

G35   In a system with a device generating 400 interrupts per second, and each interrupt processing consuming 120 μs, the fraction of time the processor does useful work is _____

G36   The CPU utilization in a system with N processes waiting for I/O, where a process spends a fraction p of its time in I/O wait state, is given by _____

H. Secondary (disk) storage and file system

H1   The module of the operating system responsible for use and operations of files is called _____

H2   The _____ is the longest of the times in a disk access.

H3   The *SSTF (shortest seek time first) disk* scheduling algorithm services the request which is on a track _____ to the current R/W head position.

H4   The SSTF scheduling algorithm services the request with

_____

H5   The disk scheduling algorithm where the request with the smallest seek time is serviced next is called

_____

H6   The arm/head starts at one end of the disk, moves towards the other end, servicing requests in order until there are no more requests in that direction, then reverses direction, and services requests the other way, in the _____ algorithm.

H7   The disk head may not fully traverse the disk in the _____ disk head scheduling algorithm.

H8   The mechanism where a group of disks is treated as a single unit is called _____

H9   The surface of a magnetic disk platter is divided into concentric circular _____

H10   Each track of a magnetic disk is divided into _____

H11   The disk head scheduling algorithm which does not take into account the current position of the disk head is

_____

H12   What are the two components of positioning time of a disk head are _____ and _____

H13   A particular track number across all the platters is collectively called _____

H14   The _____ component of a disk's I/O time is dependent on the disk's RPM.

H15   The tracks of a magnetic disk platter are divided into

_____

H16   A set of disk blocks that logically belong on disk, but are kept in a portion of memory to improve performance is called

_____

H17   The swap space usually resides on the _____

H18   The disk scheduling algorithm where disk requests are serviced as they arrive is called _____

H19   The smallest block that can be read or written on a disk is called

_____

H20   The components of a disk read/write time are _____, _____, and _____

H21   The _____ is the longest of the times in a disk access.

H22   Each file is a linked list of disk blocks in _____ allocation.

H23   Insertion and deletion of blocks in a file is easy in _____ allocation of disk blocks in a file system.

H24   Support for *very* large files is provided by _____ allocation.

H25   The _____ disk head scheduling does not take into account the current position of the disk head.

H26   The scheme for deciding the order in which disk access requests are serviced is called _____

H27   A set of physical disk drives viewed as a single logical unit by the OS is called _____

H28   The number of RAID levels are numbered _____ to
_____

H29   Blocks level striping, but without any redundancy (parity) is used
in RAID level _____

H30   Disk mirroring is used in RAID level _____

H31   Striping at the level of bytes is used in RAID level _____

H32   Bit-interleaved parity organization is used in RAID level
_____

H33   Block-interleaved parity organization is used in RAID level
_____

H34   A separate disk for parity for the blocks from other disks is used
in RAID level _____

H35   Block-interleaved distributed parity is used in RAID level
_____

H36   Block-level interleaving is used in RAID levels _____ and
_____

H37   Multiple disk failures is handled in RAID level _____

H38   For each block, one of the disks stores the parity and the others
store data in RAID level _____

H39   Error-correcting codes (such as the Reed-Solomon codes) are used
in RAID level _____

H40   The average *rotational latency* (½ of the time in seconds for one
rotation the disk) of a disk drive with 7,200 RPM (rotations per
minute) is _____

H41   The number of bytes in a *cylinder* of a disk drive with 5 platters,
each with 2 surfaces, 27,000 tracks per surface, 512 sectors per
track, and 512 bytes per sector, is _____

H42   Given a disk queue holding requests to the following cylinders (tracks) **116,22,3,11,75,185,100,87**, in order, and that the disk head is currently at cylinder (track) 88, using FCFS, the total head movement (no. of tracks traversed) is _____, and the average head movement is _____

H43   Given a disk queue holding requests to the following cylinders (tracks) **116,22,3,11,75,185,100,87**, in order, and that the disk head is currently at cylinder (track) 88, using SSTF (shortest seek time first), the total head movement (number of tracks traversed) is _____, and the average head movement is _____

H44   Given a disk queue holding requests to the following cylinders (tracks) **116,22,3,11,75,185,100,87**, in order, and that the disk head is currently at cylinder (track) 88, using SSTF (shortest seek time first), the order in which the requests are serviced is _____

H45   Given a disk queue holding requests to the following cylinders (tracks) **116,22,3,11,75,185,100,87**, in order, and that the disk head is currently at cylinder (track) 88, using C-SCAN, the total head movement (no. of tracks traversed) is _____, and the average head movement is _____

H46   Given a disk queue holding requests to the following cylinders (tracks) **116,22,3,11,75,185,100,87**, in order, and that the disk head is currently at cylinder (track) 88, using C-SCAN, the order in which the requests are serviced is

_____

H47   In constant linear velocity disk drive, the density of track is _____ going from outer tracks to inner tracks.

H48   In constant angular velocity disk drive, the density of track is _____ going from the _____ tracks to the _____ tracks.

IOIOIOIOIOIOIOIOIOIOIOIOIOIOIOIOIOIOIOIOIOIOIOIOI

Answers

(True/False)

A. Introduction and OS structure

A1   On power up, the bootstrap program is first run. ***True***

A2   The bootstrap loader brings the *entire* operating system into memory. ***False***

A3   The kernel initializes the CPU registers, device controllers, and memory. ***False***

A4   The entire operating system (such as Linux) will fit in the main memory. ***False***

A5   Most systems store only a small portion of the bootstrap loader program in the ROM/EEPROM. ***True***

A6   The operating system kernel consists of all system and application programs in a computer. ***False***

A7   Flash memory is slower than DRAM but needs no power to retain its contents. ***True***

A8   A *boot block* cannot be more than just one physical sector. ***False***

A9   A *command interpreter* is an example of a systems program. ***True***

A10   A *Web browser* is an example of a systems program. ***False***

A11   Location of boot blocks on the disk are not fixed. ***False***

A12   Most modern operating systems provide support for symmetric multiprocessing (SMP). ***True***

A13   All of Operating System needs to be in memory for proper execution. ***False***

A14   A program, as an executable file residing on disk, is static. ***True***

A15   System programs are part of the kernel. ***False***

A16   System programs are associated with the operating system. ***True***

A17 Application programs are not associated with the operating of the system. ***True***

A18 An initial small bootstrap program is located in the random-access memory (RAM). ***False***

A19 Most modern operating systems are implemented (coded) using a high-level language. ***True***

A20 Code / software to control I/O devices is (usually) not part of the operating system. ***True***

A21 Not *all* parts of an operating system can be implemented in a high-level language. ***True***

A22 Implementing the operating system in a high-level language facilitates portability. ***True***

A23 It is possible to run applications which are larger than can fit in the physical memory (RAM). ***True***

A24 Main Memory (RAM) is volatile memory. ***True***

A25 An operating system supporting more than one processor is called multiprogramming. ***False***

A26 Multiprogramming increases CPU utilization. ***True***

A27 Turning off interrupts can be done in user mode. ***False***

A28 Reading the system clock can be done in user mode. ***True***

A29 User programs can set the mode bit. ***False***

A30 All of Operating System needs to be in memory for proper execution. ***False***

A31 User programs can set the mode bit. ***False***

A32 A multicore system allows two (or more) threads that are in compute cycles to execute at the same time. ***True***

A33 In an SMP-type system each processor performs all tasks within the operating system. ***True***

A34 In a peer-to-peer systems, clients may sometimes act as servers. ***True***

A35 Kernel supported threads can be scheduled independently. ***True***

A36 The microkernel approach facilitates ease of extending the operating system. ***True***

A37 In the microkernel approach, addition of new services requires modification of the kernel. ***False***

A38 The microkernel approach facilitates ease of portability of the operating system. ***True***

A39 In the microkernel approach, all new services are added to user space. ***True***

A40 The microkernel approach, most services run as kernel services. ***False***

A41 The microkernel approach does not provide more security and reliability. ***False***

A42 Shared memory is better suited to IPC (inter-process communication) mechanism than message passing for distributed systems. ***False***

A43 A message-passing model is faster than the shared memory model. ***False***

A44 A message-passing model is better suited than a shared memory model for communication between computers. ***True***

A45 CPU executes with very limited capability in user mode. ***True***

A46 A system call is initiated by hardware. ***False***

A47 Mechanisms for process synchronization are provided by the operating system. ***True***

A48 The entire executable code of a process need not reside in memory (RAM). ***True***

A49 The OS strives to keep the CPU running all the time. ***True***

A50 The entire operating system must reside in the memory (RAM) for correct operation. *False*

A51 A job mix with more I/O-bound processes than compute-bound processes has (comparatively) lower CPU utilization. *True*

A52 System calls are usually invoked by using software interrupts. *True*

A53 Application programmers typically use an API rather than directory invoking system calls. *True*

A54 Shared memory is typically faster than message passing. *True*

A55 Message passing is typically faster than shared memory. *False*

A56 Message passing is better suited compared to shared memory for exchanging large amounts of data. *False*

A57 The operating system in a modern single user PC/laptop is not a multiprogramming OS. *False*

A58 In a modern single user PC/laptop several processes will be running even when the user has no running programs/applications. *True*

A59 The microkernel communicates with devices. *False*

A60 A microkernel provides only inter-process communication and access control. *True*

A61 Applications divided into separate tasks can run in parallel on the different cores. *True*

A62 In multicore systems data must also be divided to make them accessible by the tasks running on separate cores. *True*

A63 A *multiprogramming* system must have more than one CPU. *False*

A64 A *multiprocessing* (or *multiprocessor*) system must have two or more processors. *True*

A65   Even a single user system (such as desktop or laptop) is a *multiprogramming* system. ***True***

A66   Concurrency is only possible with parallelism. ***False***

A67   The CPU checks for a pending interrupt at the end of every few instructions. ***False***

A68   The CPU checks the interrupt line at the end of every instruction. ***True***

A69   At the end of every instruction, the CPU checks to see if the interrupt line is asserted. ***True***

A70   In a multiprogramming OS, the CPU *waits* for I/O of a process to complete before resuming execution. ***False***

A71   A real-time process may get a disproportionate share of the resources. ***True***

A72   The CPU will not use all the features provided by the hardware while executing in user mode. ***True***

A73   A *trap* instruction switches the execution mode of a CPU from user mode to kernel mode. ***True***

A74   All interrupts result in context switches. ***True***

A75   All context switches are due to interrupts. ***False***

A76   *Context switch* time does not affect the overall performance. ***False***

A77   A *non-preemptive* kernel is essentially free from race conditions. ***True***

A78   A thread making a change to a shared global variable is visible to other cooperating threads. ***True***

A79   Starting addresses of exception handlers are also (usually) stored in the same table as those of interrupt handlers. ***True***

A80   An interrupt could be caused by a condition within a processor. ***False***

A81   Concurrent execution of processes/threads must require multiple processors/cores. *False*

A82   A process modifying a kernel data structure can be interrupted. *False*

A83   Modification of a kernel data structure cannot be done in user mode. *True*

A84   Interrupts can have different priorities. *True*

A85   CPU switches to kernel mode upon any interrupt or exception. *True*

A86   Dynamic loading facilitates better memory utilization. *True*

A87   With dynamic loading the entire program does not have to be stored in main memory. *True*

A88   Normal programs run at a level above the lowest interrupt priority. *False*

A89   Attempt to execute an illegal instruction generates an interrupt. *False*

A90   Some interrupt handlers are run in user mode. *False*

A91   Too many context switches would adversely affect the throughput. *True*

A92   Handling (processing) of any interrupt is never interrupted. *False*

A93   The kernel/user mode bit can be set by the user process. *False*

A94   An executable program is always loaded in the same memory location at every invocation. *False*

A95   The bootstrap program is typically larger than one disk block. *True*

A96   Interrupts generated by devices are given higher priority than traps generated by the user program. *True*

A97   Code used for handling system calls can never be interrupted. *False*

A98   A faster CPU may not always ensure improved CPU utilization. ***True***

A99   Increasing the degree of multiprogramming always improved the CPU utilization. ***False***

A100   The check for a pending interrupt is done at the end of finishing every instruction. ***True***

A101   *Aging* is used to ensure that jobs in the lower-level queues will eventually complete their execution. ***True***

A102   A context switch takes place at every system call. ***True***

A103   A reentrant program cannot be called recursively. ***False***

A104   Parts of reentrant code can be altered during execution. ***False***

A105   A multiprogramming operating system must have more than one CPU. ***False***

A106   The degree of multiprogramming is the number of processes in the ready queue. ***False***

A107   Before proceeding to execution of the interrupt service routine (ISR), the OS disables interrupts. ***True***

A108   Shared memory is a preferred method of communication when processes are in two different machines. ***False***

A109   Providing APIs (Applications Programmer Interface) to system calls facilitate portability of programs across systems. ***True***

A110   Accessing an out-of-bounds memory location causes an interrupt. ***False***

A111   Interrupts are disabled while running an interrupt service routine (ISR). ***True***

A112   Static (non-shared) libraries can be linked with object files before run-time. ***True***

A113   There are no additional run-time loading costs for non-shared (static) libraries. ***True***

A114   Traps can be generated intentionally by a user program. ***True***

A115   User programs have no control over when an interrupt occurs. ***True***

A116   Increasing the degree of multiprogramming results in increased CPU utilization. ***True***

A117   A high level of CPU utilization and a low level of disk usage calls for reduction of the degree of multiprogramming. ***False***

A118   An executable program is never in main memory (RAM) unless it has been invoked (started). ***True***

A119   A process (a program that has been invoked) is always in main memory and *never* present on the disk. ***False***

A120   Access to a memory location which is out of bounds for the process causes an interrupt. ***False***

A121   Attempt to execute an illegal instruction (OP code) causes an exception (trap). ***True***

A122   System calls can be run in either user mode or kernel mode. ***False***

A123   Issuing a trap instruction can happen in user mode. ***True***

A124   Turning off interrupts can be done in user mode. ***False***

A125   Switching from user to kernel mode must be done in kernel (supervisory) mode. ***False***

A126   Attempt to perform an illegal memory access causes an interrupt. ***False***

A127   Attempt to execute an illegal instruction causes a trap. ***True***

A128   Most systems ignore some interrupts in order to allow a critical instruction to execute without interruption. ***True***

A129   It is possible to create a thread library without any kernel-level support. ***True***

A130   A multicore system allows two (or more) threads that are in compute cycles to execute at the same time. ***True***

A131   Relocation register is used to check for invalid memory addresses generated by a CPU. ***False***

A132   With the use of interrupt mechanism, the processor has to wait for the duration of I/O, without executing instructions from any other process. ***False***

A133   Increasing the main memory (RAM) size (generally) improves the CPU utilization. ***True***

A134   There is no instruction that cannot be interrupted. ***False***

A135   A multi-core system requires each core to have its own cache memory. ***False***

A136   A message-passing model is easier to implement than a shared memory model for inter-computer communication. ***True***

A137   The message passing is faster than shared memory for communication between computers/processors. ***False***

A138   System calls can sometimes be run in either user mode. ***False***

A139   Message passing is more commonly used for exchanging large amounts of data. ***False***

A140   Upon an interrupt, a running processes never goes to waiting state. ***True***

A141   Degree of multiprogramming refers to the number of cores in a CPU. ***False***

A142   The degree of multiprogramming increases with increase in memory (RAM). ***False***

A143   A process cannot be moved from one memory location to another during execution. ***False***

A144   Dynamic linked libraries (DLLs) link to an application at compile time. ***False***

A145   Dynamic linked library (DLL) is loaded onto RAM and run only as needed. ***True***

B. Processes and threads

B1   The parent and child processes never share (a segment of) memory. *False*

B2   The kernel has knowledge of user-level threads. *False*

B3   Every user-level thread must belong to a process. *True*

B4   Every kernel-level thread need not be associated with a process. *True*

B5   Two or more processes cannot be concurrently running the same executable program. *False*

B6   A context switch can never be voluntary (initiated by the running process). *False*

B7   A process in user mode cannot execute certain privileged hardware instructions. *True*

B8   Termination of a running process will always result in context switch. *True*

B9   A timer interrupt will result in involuntary context switch. *True*

B10   The context switch happening to a process due to an interrupt is considered voluntary. *False*

B11   A process will have a context switch every time it enters kernel mode from user mode. *False*

B12   A context switch always results in swapping. *False*

B13   A running process requesting an I/O operation results in a context switch. *True*

B14   Upon a page fault a process always blocks. *True*

B15   A page fault always results in swapping out of a page. *False*

B16   The clock interrupt can never be disabled. *False*

B17   It is possible for a process to go directly from *waiting* state to *running* state. ***False***

B18   A running process can never go to the *ready* state without first going to the *waiting* state. ***False***

B19   It is possible for a process to go directly from *ready* state to *finished* state. ***False***

B20   A process can never go to the *waiting* state from the *ready* state. ***True***

B21   A process could go to the *finished* state from *waiting* state. ***False***

B22   A process can never go to the *running* state from the *ready* state. ***False***

B23   A process can never go to the *finished* state from the *waiting* state. ***True***

B24   A process always goes to the *ready* state from the *waiting* state. ***True***

B25   A process can never go to the *finished* state from the *ready* state. ***True***

B26   A process could go to the *running* state from the *waiting* state. ***False***

B27   A process can never go to the *running* state from the *waiting* state. ***True***

B28   A process always go to the *finished* state from the *running* state. ***False***

B29   An executing process must be in memory (RAM). ***True***

B30   A process not currently executing, but in ready state, need not be in memory (RAM). ***False***

B31   After the **fork()** system call, the parent process and the child process share the data, stack and heap areas. ***False***

B32   A traditional (or heavyweight) process has a single thread of control. ***True***

B33   A thread is composed of a thread ID, program counter, register set, and heap. ***False***

B34   Each thread has its own register set and stack. ***True***

B35   A benefit of a thread pool is to reduce the overhead of repeated thread creation. ***True***

B36   It is possible to create a thread library without any kernel-level support. ***True***

B37   Thread Libraries provide APIs for creating and managing user-level threads. ***True***

B38   Different user-level threads of a process can be scheduled to run on separate processors. ***False***

B39   The kernel manages user-level threads. ***False***

B40   Every user-level thread is associated with a process. ***True***

B41   The kernel manages only the kernel-level threads. ***True***

B42   Multiple user-level threads on a multiprocessor system provide better performance than on a single-processor system. ***False***

B43   When a kernel thread blocks inside the kernel it could be swapped out. ***True***

B44   Multiple kernel-level threads can be run on multiple processors. ***True***

B45   With the number of kernel threads equal to the number of processors, the processors are guaranteed to be kept busy all the time. ***False***

B46   In a single CPU system, multiple processes can be in the *waiting* state. ***True***

B47   In a single CPU system, only one process can be in the *running* state. ***True***

B48   In a single CPU system, only one process can be in the *ready* state. ***False***

B49   In a single CPU multiprogramming system, multiple processes can be executing at any time. ***False***

B50   In a single CPU multiprogramming system, multiple processes can be resident in memory at any time. ***True***

B51   In a single CPU system, multiple processes can be in the waiting state at the same time. ***True***

B52   It is possible for a process to go directly to the *running* state from *waiting* state. ***False***

B53   Upon interrupt by a higher priority process, the process in *running* state goes to *waiting* state. ***False***

B54   Lengths of the subsequent CPU bursts of processes are known exactly in advance. ***False***

B55   The program in *reentrant code* cannot be shared among processes. ***False***

B56   The data in *reentrant code* can be shared among processes. ***False***

B57   Heap memory and global variables are shared among the threads of a multithreaded process. ***True***

B58   In a single CPU system, only one process can be in the *running* state. ***True***

B59   In a single CPU system, only one process can be in the *ready* state. ***False***

B60   Two *independent* processes can affect each other. ***False***

B61   Shared–memory is a means of inter–process communication. ***True***

B62   After the **fork()** system call, the parent process and the child process share the data, stack and heap areas. ***False***

B63   Each process executes its own *critical section*. ***True***

B64   After the **fork()** system call, the parent process and the child process share the data, stack and heap areas. *__False__*

B65   The kernel manages only the kernel-level threads. *__True__*

B66   Switching between user level threads requires kernel intervention. *__False__*

B67   Kernel threads are slower to create and manage compared to user threads. *__True__*

B68   In the *many-to-one* model, multiple user threads can access the kernel at the same time. *__False__*

B69   In the *many-to-one* model, the entire process will not block if a thread makes a blocking system call. *__False__*

B70   In the *many-to-one* model, multiple threads are unable to run in parallel on multiprocessors. *__True__*

B71   The *many-to-one* model provides more concurrency than the *one-to-one* model. *__False__*

B72   In the *one-to-one* model, another (user) thread can run when a (user) thread makes a blocking system call. *__True__*

B73   In the *many-to-many* model, N user level threads can map to more than N user level threads. *__False__*

B74   In the *many-to-many* model, N user level threads cannot map to less than N user level threads. *__False__*

B75   In the *one-to-one* model, multiple threads are unable to run in parallel on multiprocessors. *__False__*

B76   In the *many-to-many* model, multiple threads are able to run in parallel on multiprocessors. *__True__*

B77   Implementing inter-process communication is easier than implementing inter-thread communication. *__False__*

B78   A process goes from the running state to the ready state when an interrupt occurs. *__True__*

B79   Threads cannot use their own stack, other than that of the parent. ***False***

B80   A thread cannot have its own program counter. ***False***

B81   A thread has the same address space as its process. ***True***

B82   Threads of the same process can share the same stack. ***False***

B83   Each process can have its own address space. ***True***

B84   A process may span multiple pages. ***True***

B85   After a process spawns a child process, the parent and child continue to execute the same set of instructions from that point onwards. ***True***

B86   After a process spawns a child process, the order of execution of the instructions in the parent and child processes is indeterminate. ***True***

B87   Just after a child process is created, is a duplicate of the parent. ***True***

B88   Just after a child process is created, it does not run concurrently with the parent. ***False***

B89   After a child process is created, it usually has a new program loaded into it. ***True***

B90   A newly admitted process will be in running state. ***False***

B91   In the *many-to-one* mapping of user threads to kernel threads, if one user thread blocks, the other threads belonging to the same process can continue to run. ***False***

B92   In the *one-to-one* mapping of user threads to kernel threads, there is a working set for each thread of a multi-threaded process. ***True***

B93   After an I/O event is completed, a process goes to *running* state. ***False***

B94   After an I/O event is completed, a process goes to *terminated* state. ***False***

B95   Switching threads causes a trap to the kernel. ***False***

B96   Even if one user level thread of a process blocks, the entire process blocks. ***True***

B97   If one kernel level thread of a process blocks, another thread can continue execution. ***True***

B98   Management of user level threads is done by the kernel. ***False***

B99   Switching between user and kernel modes takes more time than switching between two processes. ***False***

B100   Communication between processors on a multi-core chip is faster than processors on separate chips. ***True***

B101   A process may completely be residing on the disk (secondary memory). ***True***

B102   A process must always reside in main memory (RAM). ***False***

B103   Contemporary operating systems support kernel threads. ***True***

B104   Kernel threads are generally no more expensive to maintain than user threads. ***False***

B105   Kernel threads need not be associated with a process. ***True***

B106   A web server a typically run as a single-threaded process. ***False***

B107   A web server that runs as a single-threaded process can serve only one client. ***True***

B108   A multithreaded program can allow the program to run even if part of it is blocked. ***True***

B109   The threads of a process do not share the resources belonging to the process. ***False***

B110   Multiple user-level threads of a process can run on multiple processors. ***False***

B111   A thread can be run on any processor when multiple processors are available. *True*

B112   Multiple kernel-level threads of the same process can run on multiple processors simultaneously. *True*

B113   A thread library could be implemented to reside in user space or kernel space. *True*

B114   A kernel-level thread library is supported directly by the operating system. *True*

B115   A kernel-level thread library the code and data structures exist in kernel space. *True*

B116   A thread pool avoids the overhead of repeated creation of new threads. *True*

B117   The code, data, and files are shared across the threads of the same process. *True*

B118   The threads of a process share the set of registers and the stack. *False*

B119   Stack is not shared by threads of the same process. *True*

B120   A thread cannot have its own stack, other than that of the parent process. *False*

B121   All threads of a process share the same code. *True*

B122   All threads of a process do not share the same data. *False*

B123   Blocking one kernel level thread blocks all related threads. *False*

B124   More memory requested (dynamically) by a running process is allocated on the stack. *False*

B125   Kernel support is required for the creation and destruction of user-level threads. *False*

B126   A process that is waiting for an event to occur must necessarily do a spinlock. *False*

B127   When a process does a spinlock, there will necessarily be a context switch. *False*

B128   A process waiting in some waiting queue for an event to occur will not expend CPU time. *True*

B129   Aging involves gradually increasing the priority of a process. *True*

B130   In a livelock situation, a process will eventually get to run on the CPU. *False*

B131   Use of aging allows a low priority process to use the CPU in the presence of higher priority processes. *True*

B132   Interrupt processing is done in user mode. *False*

B133   An interrupt is *never* deferred. *False*

B134   Even in a single user system, multiple processes could be in different states of execution at any time. *True*

B135   Traps can be generated due to some effects of instruction executions within a process. *True*

B136   The interrupted process is always *immediately* resumed after servicing the interrupt. *False*

B137   A thread can be scheduled and executed independently of its parent process. *True*

B138   Multithreaded programs facilitate increase of CPU usage. *True*

B139   A thread may sometimes be run on only a selected processor even when multiple processors are available. *True*

B140   The time taken to switch between user and kernel modes of execution is less than the context switch time. *True*

B141   Allocating a process all its resources before beginning its execution improves resource utilization. *False*

B142   A kernel thread does not have its own address space. *True*

B143   Thread-specific data generated by the thread is independent of the thread's process. ***True***

B144   The OS does not maintain a separate stack for each thread. ***False***

B145   Context switch is faster with kernel-supported threads. ***False***

B146   Switching among threads (of the same process) is no more efficient than switching among processes. ***False***

B147   A high-priority process which is ready, would never have to wait while a low-priority process is running. ***False***

B148   After an I/O event is completed, a process goes to the *running* state. ***False***

B149   Several processes can be running in kernel mode. ***True***

B150   Most modern operating systems swap entire processes to swap space. ***False***

C. CPU Scheduling

C1   Typically the scheduler gives higher preference to CPU-bound processes to run on the CPU compared to I/O-bound processes. ***False***

C2   Typically the I/O-bound processes do not use up their quantum of time. ***True***

C3   The CPU bursts of compute-bound processes are typically larger than those of I/O-bound processes. ***True***

C4   Having I/O-bound processes use the CPU ahead of compute-bound processes reduces the average wait time of processes. ***True***

C5   Reducing the context-switch frequency tends to increase the average response time of processes. ***True***

C6   Reducing the context-switch frequency tends to decrease the CPU utilization. ***False***

C7   The SJF scheduling could lead to starvation. ***True***

C8   The RR scheduling could lead to starvation. ***False***

C9   The RR scheduling is non-preemptive. ***False***

C10   The RR scheduling could lead to starvation. ***False***

C11   The permanent assignment of a process to a particular queue in a multilevel feedback-queue system provides more flexibility. ***False***

C12   A process entering a multilevel feedback queue is usually placed in the (lower priority) FCFS queue. ***False***

C13   The Shortest Job First (SJF) scheduling could lead to starvation. ***True***

C14   The Shortest Job First (SJF) scheduling is non-preemptive. ***True***

C15   The Shortest Remaining Time (SRT) scheduling is non-preemptive. ***False***

C16   The RR scheduling could lead to starvation. *__False__*

C17   The RR scheduling is non-preemptive. *__False__*

C18   The FCFS scheduling scheme will never lead to starvation. *__True__*

C19   The Shortest Job First (SJF) scheduling would not lead to starvation. *__False__*

C20   The RR scheduling will never lead to starvation. *__True__*

C21   In RR scheduling, a running job can never be interrupted. *__False__*

C22   In Round-robin (RR) scheduling, the time-quantum should be small with respect to the context-switch time. *__False__*

C23   The most complex scheduling algorithm is the multilevel feedback-queue algorithm. *__True__*

C24   Round-robin (RR) scheduling degenerates to first-come-first-served (FCFS) scheduling if the time-quantum is too long. *__True__*

C25   The FCFS scheduling scheme could lead to starvation. *__False__*

C26   CPU bursts are predicted based on past behavior (CPU usage pattern). *__True__*

C27   The different levels of a multilevel queue system must have the same time-quantum. *__False__*

C28   Scheduling with larger time-quantum generally requires fewer context switches. *__True__*

C29   A high priority process in a real–time system runs in non–preemptive mode. *__True__*

C30   Starvation is not an issue in priority scheduling. *__False__*

C31   Starvation is an issue in round robin (RR) scheduling. *__False__*

C32   Starvation is not an issue in first-come-first-served (FCFS) scheduling. *__True__*

C33   Starvation is not an issue in shortest job first scheduling. *__False__*

C34   Starvation is an issue in shortest remaining time first scheduling. **_True_**

C35   Priority scheduling gives the minimum average waiting time. **_False_**

C36   Shortest job first (SJF) scheduling gives the minimum average waiting time. **_True_**

C37   Multiple-level queues is not really a separate scheduling algorithm. **_True_**

C38   Shortest remaining time (SRT) is a non-preemptive process scheduling algorithm. **_False_**

C39   Earliest deadline first (EDF) is a preemptive process scheduling algorithm. **_True_**

C40   The long-term scheduler selects a _mix_ of CPU-bound and I/O-bound jobs. **_True_**

C41   Short (CPU time) processes are disadvantaged in FCFS scheduling. **_True_**

C42   In round-robin scheduling jobs can get different quanta of time. **_False_**

C43   In round-robin scheduling, the time-quantum should be large compared to context switch time. **_True_**

C44   Round-robin scheduling is not well suited for real-time systems. **_True_**

C45   FCFS scheduling is well suited for real-time systems. **_False_**

C46   Preemptive scheduling is well suited for real-time systems. **_True_**

C47   Preemptive scheduling may cause starvation. **_True_**

C48   Shortest remaining time first scheduling will not cause starvation. **_False_**

C49   FCFS provides better response time than round robin scheduling. **_False_**

C50   Increasing the time-quantum would result in decreased average turnaround time. ***False***

C51   Increasing the time-quantum would result in increased average waiting time. ***True***

C52   In non–preemptive scheduling, *every* process runs to completion without being taken out of the CPU. ***False***

C53   In multilevel queue scheduling, a newly entering process is placed in the *lowest priority* queue. ***False***

C54   In non-preemptive scheduling a process can continue to run till it finishes execution. ***False***

C55   In non-preemptive scheduling a process can continue to run till it finishes with its current CPU burst. ***True***

C56   Each of the queues in multi-level feedback queue scheduling must have the same scheduling algorithm. ***False***

C57   A multi-level feedback queue scheduler generally assigns a long quantum to low priority processes. ***True***

C58   In round robin (RR) scheduling, when the quantum is small, there will be more context switches. ***True***

C59   *Convoy effect* can happen only in non–preemptive scheduling. ***True***

C60   *Convoy effect* can happen even in preemptive scheduling. ***False***

C61   In multilevel queue scheduling, processes can move between queues. ***True***

C62   Processes can move across queues in a multilevel feedback queue system. ***True***

C63   The context switch overhead increases when the RR time-quantum is increased. ***False***

C64   The terms *process scheduler* and *CPU scheduler* refer to different things. ***False***

C65   The CPU scheduler is not present in a single CPU system. ***False***

C66   In preemptive scheduling, the sections of code affected by interrupts must be guarded from simultaneous use. ***True***

C67   Process scheduler can move a job from running to waiting state. ***False***

C68   In a single CPU system, the *first in first out* scheduling results in the minimum average waiting time. ***False***

C69   Increasing the time-quantum in round-robin CPU scheduling, always results in increased turn-around time. ***False***

C70   Preemption is a 'must' for interactive systems. ***True***

C71   While switching context from process *A* to process *B*, the process *A* is always swapped out. ***False***

C72   The CPU scheduler can interrupt a running process. ***False***

C73   In *Little's formula*, λ represents the average waiting time in the queue. ***False***

C74   Predicting the next CPU burst of processes is not relevant in first-come-first-served (FCFS) scheduling. ***True***

C75   Predicting the next CPU burst of processes is needed in round robin (RR) scheduling. ***False***

D. Process synchronization

D1 Race condition refers to the indeterminate nature of the order of executions of a set of (assembly/machine language) statements. ***True***

D2 Synchronization among cooperative processes is necessitated by data sharing. ***True***

D3 Use of semaphores, no matter in what order the programmer uses, guarantee proper synchronization. ***False***

D4 Semaphores are used for controlled access to both critical section as well as to shared resources. ***True***

D5 The *entry section* ensures that the conditions are right for the process to enter it's *critical section*. ***True***

D6 Each of the cooperating processes has its own *critical section*. ***True***

D7 *Binary semaphores* cannot be used for the critical-section problem for multiple processes. ***False***

D8 Race condition can occur only in multiprocessor systems. ***False***

D9 Race conditions are prevented by requiring that critical regions be protected by locks. ***True***

D10 All solutions to the critical section problem are based on some form of locking. ***True***

D11 Multiple processes can be executing their critical sections at the same time. ***False***

D12 The *Test-and-Set* instruction should be executed atomically (without interruption). ***True***

D13 The *semaphore* used for synchronization of two (or more) processes need not be a shared variable. ***False***

D14 In a normal system, more than one of concurrent processes could execute in their *critical regions*. ***False***

D15   Synchronization of concurrent processes may not guarantee the same (consistent) results when executed at different times. *False*

D16   Synchronization is not required among concurrent processes which do not share resources. *True*

D17   A *semaphore* is essentially an integer variable. *True*

D18   A semaphore can be modified simultaneously by multiple threads. *False*

D19   A semaphore is a shared variable (memory location). *True*

D20   Semaphores cannot provide the same functionality as mutex locks. *False*

D21   A process typically spends a small percentage of its time in its critical section. *True*

D22   The variable shared among cooperating processes is accessed/updated in the *critical section*. *True*

D23   Each of the concurrent cooperating processes has its own *critical section*. *True*

D24   The value of *any* semaphore can range only between 0 and 1. *False*

D25   Process *starvation* is not possible while using semaphores. *False*

D26   In the *Readers–Writers* problem, more than one reader can be reading simultaneously. *True*

D27   In the *readers–writers* problem, the semaphore that ensures mutual exclusion between the writer and reader processes must be a counting semaphore. *False*

D28   A counting semaphore can never be used as a binary semaphore. *False*

D29   A binary semaphore can never be used as a counting semaphore. *True*

D30   A counting semaphore can be simulated using multiple binary semaphores. *True*

D31   Spinlocks can be used to prevent busy waiting in the implementation of semaphore. *False*

D32   Counting semaphores can be used to control access to a resource with a finite number of instances. *True*

D33   A semaphore can be used to control access to a thread's critical sections. *True*

D34   The value of a counting semaphore can range only between 0 and 1. *False*

D35   The local variables of a monitor can be accessed by only the local procedures. *True*

D36   The semaphore in the producer–consumer problem which controls access to the shared buffer could be a binary semaphore. *True*

D37   The semaphore used to ensure mutual exclusive access to critical section by two (or more) processes need not be a shared variable. *False*

D38   The exact order of executions of statements of concurrent processes could be different when executed at different times. *True*

D39   Even with synchronization, concurrent processes could produce different results when executed at different times. *False*

D40   Synchronization of concurrent processes guarantees the same (consistent) results even when executed at different times. *True*

D41   A process typically spends a small percentage of its time in its critical region. *True*

D42   A binary semaphore can be used when there is no more than one resource. *True*

D43   Semaphores can be simulated using monitors. *True*

D44   Monitors cannot be simulated using semaphores. *False*

D45   A binary semaphore which is initialized to 1 will never be negative when working properly. **_True_**

D46   If a process using a binary semaphore invokes the `signal` operation in its entry section, and the `wait` operation in its exit section, multiple processes could be in their critical sections. **_True_**

D47   If a process using a binary semaphore invokes the `wait` operation in its entry section, and the `wait` operation in its exit section, none of the other processes could be in their critical sections. **_True_**

D48   In a system with two processes P_1 and P_2, and a binary semaphore, S used for accessing a critical section, if P_2 is missing `signal(S)`, then P_1 can still enter its critical section. **_False_**

D49   In a system with two processes P_1 and P_2, and a binary semaphore, S used for accessing a critical section, if P_2 is missing `signal(S)`, then P_2 cannot enter its critical section the second time around. **_True_**

D50   In a system with two concurrent processes $P1$ and $P2$ synchronized using a binary semaphore S, when $P2$ is in its critical section, $P1$ cannot be in its exit section. **_True_**

D51   In a system with two concurrent processes $P1$ and $P2$ synchronized using a binary semaphore S, when $P2$ is in its critical section, $P1$ can be in its entry section. **_True_**

D52   In a system with two concurrent processes $P1$ and $P2$ synchronized using a binary semaphore S, when $P2$ is in its critical section, $P1$ can be in its remainder section. **_True_**

D53   In a system with two concurrent processes $P1$ and $P2$ synchronized using a binary semaphore S, when $P2$ is in its critical section, $P1$ can be in its critical section. **_False_**

D54   In a system with two concurrent processes $P1$ and $P2$ synchronized using a binary semaphore S, when $P1$ is in its entry section, $P2$ can be in its entry section. **_True_**

D55   In a system with two concurrent processes $P1$ and $P2$ synchronized using a binary semaphore S, when $P1$ is in its exit section, $P2$ cannot be in its entry section. ***False***

D56   In a system with two concurrent processes $P1$ and $P2$ synchronized using a binary semaphore S, when $P1$ is in its exit section, $P2$ can be in its exit section. ***False***

D57   In a system with two concurrent processes $P1$ and $P2$ synchronized using a binary semaphore S, when $P1$ is in its remainder section, $P2$ can be in its remainder section. ***True***

D58   Process *deadlock* is a possibility while using semaphores. ***True***

D59   The *semaphore* used to ensure mutual exclusive access to critical section by two (or more) processes need not be a shared variable. ***False***

D60   The *semaphore* used for synchronization must be a shared variable. ***True***

D61   In the *readers–writers* problem, each reader process has exclusive access to the buffer. ***False***

D62   In the *readers–writers* problem, the reader and writer processes have exclusive access to the buffer. ***True***

D63   In the *readers–writers* problem, multiple reader processes can access the buffer. ***True***

D64   A critical section can consist of multiple instructions. ***True***

D65   The producer-consumer problem cannot be solved using monitors. ***False***

D66   The producer-consumer problem can be solved *only* using semaphores. ***False***

D67   Only a subset of the instructions in a critical section are executed as an atomic unit (without interruption). ***False***

D68   Semaphore value is modified in the *remainder* section of the code. ***False***

D69   A semaphore need not be updated in a mutually exclusive manner. **_False_**

D70   A binary semaphore cannot be used to implement mutual exclusion among N processes. **_False_**

D71   Mutual exclusion is optional for non–sharable resources. **_False_**

D72   Mutual exclusion is required for all sharable resources. **_False_**

D73   Mutual exclusion is not required for some sharable resources. **_True_**

D74   Switching the order of execution of *wait()* and *signal()* in a process will always result in deadlock. **_False_**

D75   Switching the order of execution of *wait()* and *signal()* in a process will affect mutual exclusion. **_True_**

D76   Switching the order of execution of *wait()* and *signal()* in a process could result in several processes to be active in their critical sections at the same time. **_True_**

D77   Giving preference to multiple readers to access the shared resource (buffer) versus a single writer, increases the throughput in the *readers-writers* problem. **_True_**

D78   The number of licenses in commercial software packages indicating the number of applications that may run concurrently, can be implemented using a semaphore. **_True_**

D79   A critical section can never be nested inside another one. **_False_**

D80   In a set of cooperating processes, no assumptions may be made about speeds of the processes. **_True_**

D81   In a set of cooperating processes, more than one process cannot be in its critical section. **_True_**

D82   Using the monitor construct, only one process at a time can be active within the monitor. **_True_**

D83   A *monitor* is an object whose methods are always executed in mutual exclusion. **_True_**

D84   The variable shared across cooperating processes is updated in the *critical section*. ***True***

D85   Cooperating processes share a common critical section. ***False***

D86   Peterson's solution would work for synchronization of more than two processes. ***False***

D87   Each process executes its own *critical section*. ***True***

D88   Two independent processes can affect each other. ***False***

D89   Shared–memory is a means of inter–process communication. ***True***

D90   Allowing several threads try to access (read) the same data concurrently is allowed in many applications. ***True***

D91   An instruction which is said to execute atomically must consist of only one machine instruction. ***False***

D92   Processes that are executing in their critical sections can participate to decide on the next process to enter its critical section. ***False***

D93   Race conditions are prevented by requiring that critical sections be protected by locks. ***True***

D94   The *semaphore* used to ensure mutual exclusive access to critical section by two (or more) processes need not be a shared variable. ***False***

D95   The *critical section* is shared among cooperating processes. ***False***

D96   Semaphores used by cooperating processes must be global variables. ***True***

D97   Operations on semaphores must be done atomically. ***True***

D98   When a process starts spinlock, it continues to use the CPU. ***True***

D99   Mutex locks and counting semaphores are equivalent. ***False***

D100   Mutex locks and binary semaphores are equivalent. ***True***

D101   A process modifies the value(s) of semaphore(s) in the critical section. **_False_**

D102   Mutual exclusion will not be affected if the semaphore operations (wait and signal) are not done atomically. **_False_**

D103   The operations on a semaphore must be done atomically (mutually exclusively). **_True_**

D104   Multiple mutually disjoint processes have no need for synchronization. **_True_**

D105   Accesses (reads) to files and databases by cooperating processes must always be mutually exclusive. **_False_**

D106   Updates (writes) to files and databases by cooperating processes need not always be mutually exclusive. **_False_**

D107   A process can access/update shared data in its entry section. **_True_**

D108   The *test-and-set* instruction must execute uninterrupted for correct operation. **_True_**

D109   The *test-and-set* instruction is a single machine level instruction. **_False_**

D110   A lock that uses busy wait is called a *spinlock*. **_True_**

D111   *Busy wait* is a hindrance to efficient use of CPU. **_True_**

D112   Busy waiting can be avoided by having the processes waiting on a semaphore to enter a *blocked* state. **_True_**

D113   A spinlock is useful when locks are expected to be held for long amounts of time. **_False_**

D114   The local variables of a monitor can be accessed by only the local procedures. **_True_**

D115   Spinlocks waste CPU cycles. **_True_**

D116   Spinlocks are not appropriate for single-processor systems. **_True_**

D117   Bulk of the work of a process is done in the *critical section*. **_False_**

D118   The data streamed from a Web server to a client fits the readers-writers model. ***False***

D119   Cooperative clients accessing a database fits the producer-consumer model. ***False***

D120   Critical regions protected by locks prevents race conditions. ***True***

D121   *Mutual exclusion* is not a necessary condition for deadlock. ***False***

D122   *Hold and wait* is a necessary condition for deadlock. ***True***

D123   *No preemption* is not a necessary condition for deadlock. ***False***

D124   The *banker's algorithm* is useful in a system with single instance of each resource type. ***False***

E. Deadlocks

E1   Excessive resource usage is not a necessary condition for deadlock. ***True***

E2   In a system which is in an unsafe state, it is possible for the processes to complete their executions without getting into a deadlock. ***True***

E3   The circular-wait condition for a deadlock implies the hold-and-wait condition. ***True***

E4   Prevention is most commonly used in practice for handing deadlocks. ***False***

E5   Despite allocation of all of a job's required resources, it may still cause deadlock. ***False***

E6   Removal of any one of the four necessary conditions for deadlock prevents deadlock. ***True***

E7   If there is no circular wait (for resources) a deadlock can still occur. ***False***

E8   When a system is in the unsafe state, it will eventually lead to deadlock. ***False***

E9   A deadlock avoidance system may, at times, allow the system to enter the unsafe state. ***True***

E10   The total number of existing resources could be less than the total demands of all the processes and still maintain safety. ***True***

E11   Deadlock avoidance is less restrictive than deadlock prevention. ***True***

E12   A cycle in the resource-allocation graph with only one instance of every resource type does not necessarily indicate a deadlock situation. ***False***

E13   A job may hold onto a resource even after finishing. ***False***

E14   Allocation of even only a subset of the required resources to processes could lead to deadlock. **_True_**

E15   Allocation of all of the required resources to a process may not lead to deadlock. **_True_**

E16   *All* of the four necessary conditions for deadlock must be removed for deadlock prevention. **_False_**

E17   A circular wait for resources is not necessarily a deadlock situation. **_False_**

E18   Deadlocks can be prevented by not allowing at least one of the four necessary conditions. **_True_**

E19   The wait-for graph scheme is not applicable to a resource allocation system with multiple instances of each resource type. **_True_**

E20   The *banker's algorithm* is applicable in a system with multiple instances of each resource type. **_True_**

E21   Deadlock prevention and deadlock avoidance are essentially the same approaches for handling deadlock. **_False_**

E22   Excessive resource usage can cause deadlock. **_False_**

E23   A safe state may lead to a deadlocked state. **_False_**

E24   A safe state will never lead to a deadlocked state. **_True_**

E25   An unsafe state is always a deadlocked state. **_False_**

E26   If there is no circular wait (for resources) a deadlock can still occur. **_False_**

E27   Deadlock prevention and avoidance are the same thing for handling deadlocks. **_False_**

E28   A system in an unsafe state will eventually deadlock. **_False_**

E29   Deadlock avoidance requires knowledge of resource requirements a priori. **_True_**

E30   With only a single shared resource, a deadlock situation will not occur. ***True***

E31   All *starvation* situations are due to *deadlocks*. ***False***

E32   Database records could be shared resources. ***True***

E33   Not allocating partial list of the resources for a process may result in reduced performance. ***True***

E34   It is always possible to know in advance the resource requirements of every process. ***False***

E35   Breaking a deadlock always requires at least one victim process (to be terminated). ***True***

E36   Deadlock is not possible while the system is in a safe state. ***True***

E37   Deadlock cannot occur with spooled resources. ***False***

E38   A *safe state* ensures that there is a sequence for processes to finish their program execution. ***True***

E39   In an unsafe state there are no free resources in the system. ***False***

E40   Existence of more than zero free resources in the system guarantees that it is safe state. ***False***

E41   Removal of 'hold and wait' condition requires processes to request all the resources needed before starting. ***True***

E42   Removal of 'hold and wait' condition will not reduce the efficiency of use of resources. ***False***

E43   Releasing all resources before requesting a new resource is a valid deadlock prevention scheme. ***True***

E44   Starting execution only after obtaining all required resources will not result in the deadlock of that process. ***True***

E45   Circular wait is avoided by assigning precedence to resources and requiring processes to request resources in order of increasing precedence. ***True***

E46   Disabling interrupts during critical sections will not avoid circular waits. *False*

E47   A deadlock-avoidance scheme facilitates more concurrent use of resources than schemes that statically prevent deadlock formation (deadlock prevention). *True*

E48   A deadlock-avoidance scheme will not contribute to increased runtime overheads. *False*

E49   When the CPU wants to perform a memory read/write, it is *always* granted immediate access to memory bus. *False*

E50   Imposing a total ordering of all resource types and requiring the resources to be acquired in order, prevents deadlock from occurring. *True*

E51   Requiring a process to request resources only when it has none, will ensure *hold-and-wait* condition never occurs. *True*

E52   Requiring a process to request all its resources before the start of its execution may not guarantee that *hold-and-wait* condition never occurs. *False*

E53   Imposing a total ordering of all resource types and requiring the resources to be acquired in order, may not guarantee absence of circular-wait condition. *False*

E54   In practice, the deadlock-detection algorithm is invoked for every resource request. *False*

E55   Deadlock is still possible while the system is in a safe state. *False*

E56   Assigning a resource to a process which is in safe state may take it to an unsafe state. *True*

E57   A process is in a deadlocked state whenever it is waiting for resources that are being used by other process(es). *False*

E58   Circular wait is a necessary, but not sufficient condition for deadlock. *True*

E59   Preempting a resource is a deadlock recovery mechanism. *False*

E60   Killing one of the processes is a deadlock recovery mechanism. ***False***

E61   A cycle in the resource-allocation graph is a necessary and sufficient condition for deadlock in the case where each resource has more than one instance. ***False***

E62   A cycle in the resource-allocation graph is a necessary and sufficient condition for deadlock in the case where each resource has exactly one instance. ***True***

E63   The circular-wait condition for deadlock implies the hold-and-wait condition. ***True***

E64   In a system where each resource type contains only a single instance and the resource-allocation graph contain cycles, a deadlock exists. ***True***

E65   In case of a resource type containing more than one instance, the presence of a cycle in the resource-allocation graph does not guarantee deadlock. ***True***

E66   Not all unsafe states lead to deadlocks. ***True***

E67   In a deadlocked system, a job/process which is not deadlocked could never be chosen as the victim to be terminated. ***False***

E68   If a system does not have deadlocks, it is guaranteed not to have starvation. ***False***

E69   If a system has multiple cooperating processes, but only one shared resource then it will not have deadlocks. ***True***

E70   Deadlock would not occur if the number of resources is greater than the number of processes. ***False***

E71   If there are no cycles in the resource allocation graph, then there is no deadlock. ***True***

E72   If there are cycles in the resource allocation graph, then there is deadlock. ***False***

E73   Presence of a cycle in a *wait-for* graph indicates deadlock. ***True***

E74 A safe state ensures that there is a sequence of processes to finish their program execution. ***True***

E75 A process which is deadlocked is necessarily starved. ***True***

E76 A process which is not deadlocked is never starved. ***False***

E77 When a system has no available free resources, then it is in a deadlock state. ***False***

E78 When a system is in deadlock state, it has no available free resources. ***False***

E79 In practice, systems are designed for deadlocks never to occur. ***False***

E80 Deadlocks *never* need manual intervention. ***False***

E81 A deadlock-free solution eliminates the possibility of starvation. ***False***

E82 In the *Dining Philosophers* problem with 5 philosophers, 3 of them may eat simultaneously. ***False***

E83 If a resource-allocation graph has a cycle, the system must be in a deadlocked state. ***False***

E84 Schemes for preventing hold-and-wait conditions also prevent starvation. ***False***

E85 A deadlock-free solution eliminates the possibility of starvation. ***False***

E86 In the case of each resource having exactly one instance, a cycle in a resource-allocation graph is a necessary and sufficient condition for a deadlock. ***True***

E87 In the case of each resource having more than one instance, a cycle in a resource-allocation graph is a necessary and sufficient condition for a deadlock. ***False***

E88 The *wait-for* graph scheme is not applicable to a resource allocation system with multiple instances of each resource type. ***True***

E89   The *wait-for graph* can be used only in the case of a single instance of each resource type. ***True***

E90   Deadlocked processes can come out of deadlocked state without external intervention. ***False***

E91   A system with no available free resources always indicates a deadlocked condition. ***False***

E92   Hold and wait is not a sufficient condition for deadlock. ***True***

E93   No preemption is not a sufficient condition for deadlock. ***True***

E94   Unsafe state is a subset of deadlock state. ***False***

E95   Removal of any one condition (out of the four) is removed, the deadlock will be resolved. ***True***

E96   The *Banker's algorithm* is used for prevention of deadlocks. ***False***

E97   Multithreaded programs are not prone to deadlocks. ***False***

E98   Allocating a process all its resources before beginning its execution avoids deadlocks. ***True***

E99   Defining a linear ordering of resource types prevents circular wait. ***True***

E100   Circular wait is not a sufficient condition for deadlock. ***True***

E101   Mutual exclusion is not a sufficient condition for deadlock. ***True***

F. Memory management and virtual memory

F1   Under contiguous allocation, a running process requesting more memory (dynamically) may result in relocation of the entire process. ***True***

F2   Under pure segmentation, a running process requesting more memory (dynamically) may not result in relocation of the entire process. ***False***

F3   The contiguous memory allocation scheme does not allow processes to share code. ***True***

F4   The segmentation scheme does not allow processes to share code. ***False***

F5   The paging scheme does not allow processes to share code. ***False***

F6   Paging suffers from external fragmentation. ***False***

F7   The relocation register is used to check for invalid memory addresses generated by a CPU. ***False***

F8   The physical address space is smaller than logical (virtual) address space. ***True***

F9   Arithmetic/Logic operations can be directly performed by the CPU on memory contents. ***False***

F10   Cache memory could be as large as the main memory (RAM). ***False***

F11   The base and limit registers ensure the validity of the addresses of a process. ***True***

F12   The relocation register is used to obtain the physical memory addresses. ***True***

F13   The Best-Fit allocation scheme minimizes internal fragmentation. ***True***

F14   Paging has external fragmentation. ***False***

F15   Segmentation has external fragmentation. ***True***

F16   Segmentation has no internal fragmentation. ***True***

F17   The First-Fit allocation scheme takes a longer time to look for a free block compared to others. ***False***

F18   The logical address space is generally much larger than the physical address space. ***True***

F19   The sizes of (logical) pages and (physical) frames are different. ***False***

F20   The higher order bits of the logical address representing the page number are used to directly index the Page Table to get the frame number. ***True***

F21   The offset of a byte within a page is the same as the offset of the byte within the frame to which the page maps. ***True***

F22   The first-fit allocation method generally finds a partition faster than the best-fit allocation. ***True***

F23   The best-fit allocation method need not search for all the free blocks before an allocation. ***False***

F24   The first-fit allocation method must search for all the free blocks before an allocation. ***False***

F25   All the pages of a program/job/process need not be of the same size. ***False***

F26   The page size and the main memory frame size are of the same size. ***True***

F27   All the pages of a job/process must always reside in the main memory. ***False***

F28   All the pages of a job/process are always stored in contiguous main memory frames. ***False***

F29   A smaller page size results in a correspondingly larger page table. ***True***

F30   There are as many page tables as there are jobs/processes. ***True***

F31   The average memory access time decreases with increase in cache hit ratio. ***True***

F32   The byte offset within a memory frame is the same as the byte offset in the corresponding page. ***True***

F33   The number of entries (rows) in a page map table depends on the number of pages in the job. ***True***

F34   The CPU could sometimes bypass the cache and access the memory (RAM) directly. ***False***

F35   There is a *job table* for every active job in the system. ***False***

F36   The (page map table) PMT (or part of it) also resides in (some part of) main memory. ***True***

F37   There are situations when the PMT may not contain the frame numbers for some pages. ***True***

F38   In a PMT (Page Map Table) entry, if the *modified* field/bit is not set, then corresponding page is not written onto disk. ***True***

F39   The contents of the PMT can never change during the lifetime of a job. ***False***

F40   Pages of a given process (job) may have different sizes. ***False***

F41   All page map tables (PMTs) are of the same size. ***False***

F42   Each job/process has its own page map table. ***True***

F43   All memory frames in a system are of the same size. ***True***

F44   There are as many entries (rows) in a page map table as there are memory frames. ***False***

F45   The PMT contains the memory frame number for *every* page of a job/process. ***False***

F46   Cache memory can sometimes be as big as the main memory (RAM). ***False***

F47   Increasing the number of page frames in main memory may not reduce page faults across all page replacement algorithms. ***True***

F48   Increasing the number of page frames in main memory always reduces page faults under FIFO page replacement algorithms. ***False***

F49   There is one *valid-invalid* bit per page of logical memory. ***False***

F50   Optimal page replacement is the preferred page-replacement used in practice. ***False***

F51   Optimal page replacement algorithm keeps track of previously used pages. ***False***

F52   Optimal page replacement algorithm is impossible to implement. ***True***

F53   Optimal page replacement algorithm assumes a 'knowledge' of the future. ***True***

F54   Optimal page replacement is used as a benchmark for performance of page replacement schemes. ***True***

F55   Segments can sometimes be paged. ***True***

F56   Segmented paging is helpful when the page table is small. ***False***

F57   When large contiguous sections of the page table are unused, they can be collapsed into a single-segment table entry. ***True***

F58   Sharing a reentrant module is easier using segmentation than using pure paging. ***True***

F59   Multiple pages are never mapped onto the same hashed page table entry. ***False***

F60   The byte offset within the mapped frame is the same as the byte offset in the corresponding virtual page. ***True***

F61   The byte offset within the mapped frame could be different than the byte offset in the corresponding virtual page. ***False***

F62   Each entry of the TLB contains the (logical) page number and the corresponding (physical) frame number. ***True***

F63   The number of TLB entries depends on the (logical) page size. ***False***

F64   The number of TLB entries depends on the (physical) frame size. ***False***

F65   The number of TLB entries is independent of the logical address space. ***True***

F66   A process always blocks on a TLB miss. ***False***

F67   A page reference might have a TLB miss but no necessarily a page fault. ***True***

F68   The frame number from a page table is obtained by using the page number as an index into the page table. ***True***

F69   The number of entries in a page table depends on the number of (logical) pages. ***True***

F70   The number of entries in a page table depends on the number of (physical) frames. ***False***

F71   A page cannot be in main memory (RAM) if that page number is not in TLB. ***False***

F72   The number of entries in a TLB depends on the number of pages. ***False***

F73   The TLB entries are sorted by the virtual page numbers. ***False***

F74   In a TLB all the entries need to be searched sequentially. ***False***

F75   A page fault must be preceded by a TLB miss. ***True***

F76   A TLB miss always indicates page fault condition. ***False***

F77   In a TLB, all the entries are searched sequentially. ***False***

F78   Context switching time is typically much less than swap in/out time. ***True***

F79   Fragmentation does not occur in a paging system. ***False***

F80   On a demand-paging system, a process will experience a high page fault rate when the process begins execution. ***True***

F81   The page table entries are the addresses of frames in physical memory. ***True***

F82   Reference to a page that is not residing in main memory causes an interrupt. ***True***

F83   Segmentation has fixed-sized blocks. ***False***

F84   In paged segmentation, there are multiple memory references per page. ***True***

F85   Each process has its own page table. ***True***

F86   Inverted Page Table contains one entry per physical page frame. ***True***

F87   The number of entries in an *inverted* page table depends on the number of logical pages. ***False***

F88   Address translation under segmentation requires just two registers per segment. ***True***

F89   Segmentation has higher memory overhead in the logical to physical address translation compared to paging. ***False***

F90   In pure paging, the page table only has as many entries as there are pages of the process in the main memory. ***False***

F91   In pure paging, the page table spans all of the virtual address space of the program. ***True***

F92   Two processes having the same number of bits of logical address, but with different number of page requirements have page tables of different sizes. ***False***

F93   Programs which require more memory than is available in physical memory cannot be run. ***False***

F94   Loading only the necessary pages for execution of a process into memory will have no effect on the I/O overhead for swapping. **_False_**

F95   Demand paging increases the degree of multiprogramming. **_True_**

F96   In pure demand paging, the page fault rate is initially high. **_True_**

F97   Not requiring all of the pages of a process to be in memory increases the throughput. **_True_**

F98   Paged segmentation reduces wasted memory due to external fragmentation. **_True_**

F99   Paged segmentation reduces memory allocation time. **_True_**

F100   It is easier to share a reentrant module using paging than when using segmentation. **_False_**

F101   There cannot be a page fault when there is a TLB hit. **_True_**

F102   There is always a page fault when there is a TLB miss. **_False_**

F103   A TLB miss always results in the process being blocked. **_False_**

F104   The page table contents do not change at context switch. **_False_**

F105   The translation look-aside buffer (TLB) contents change at context switch. **_True_**

F106   Some pages of a process may be heavily used, while some rarely (or not at all). **_True_**

F107   The least recently used (LRU) is not (computationally) expensive to implement. **_False_**

F108   Extra hardware is required for the efficient implementation the LRU algorithm. **_True_**

F109   Trashing can also be a consequence of poor page replacement algorithms. **_True_**

F110   There is a separate inverted page table for every process. **_False_**

F111   Inverted page table stores the paging information of all the processes in a single table. ***True***

F112   An inverted page table stores one entry per physical frame. ***True***

F113   Very small page size is the likely cause of trashing. ***False***

F114   Far too many processes running in a system is likely cause of trashing. ***True***

F115   Virtual memory increases the degree of multiprogramming. ***True***

F116   Increasing the memory (RAM) of a system typically helps reduce the page fault rate. ***True***

F117   A large virtual address space and a small page size results in a small page table size. ***False***

F118   The minimum number of page frames that must be allocated to a running process is determined by physical memory size. ***False***

F119   A multi-level page table helps reduce the number of page faults. ***False***

F120   A multi-level page table reduces the effective memory access time. ***False***

F121   Every process has its own TLB. ***True***

F122   On a context switch, the TLB is saved on the stack. ***False***

F123   Every page entry in TLB has the corresponding page residing in a physical (main memory) frame. ***True***

F124   Every page residing in a physical (main memory) frame, may not have an entry in the TLB. ***True***

F125   Smaller page size results in larger page table size. ***True***

F126   Smaller page sizes result in larger internal fragmentation. ***False***

F127   Larger page sizes (generally) tend to reduce page faults. ***True***

F128   The entire memory image of a process must be moved from memory to disk during swap out. *False*

F129   Only selected pages of a process in memory frames are moved from memory to disk during swap out. *True*

F130   Repopulating the TLB could be a significant component of context switching. *True*

F131   On a context switch, all the entries of a tagged TLB are invalidated. *False*

F132   Hashed page tables are commonly used for handling addresses larger than 32 bits. *True*

F133   The TLB (irrespective of any additional data) must always be flushed during a context switch. *False*

F134   The size of the page table is independent of the size of the virtual address space. *False*

F135   A larger virtual address space would have a larger page table. *True*

F136   Entries in the segment table of two different jobs can never point to the same physical location. *False*

F137   A segment could belong to the address space of two different processes. *True*

F138   Lower order bits of logical address give the page number. *False*

F139   More than one (physical) frame can correspond to a given (logical) page. *False*

F140   While using segmentation, the segments may be of variable length. *True*

F141   Using segmentation, the segments must be allocated contiguously. *False*

F142   Segmentation does not suffer from external fragmentation. *False*

F143   A large page table can itself be paged. *True*

F144   A page selected for swapping out is *always* written on disk. ***False***

F145   Page table entries of two or more different processes may never have the same page number when those processes are active. ***False***

F146   The design principles of the TLB are similar to those of cache. ***True***

F147   The TLB is usually organized as fully-associative cache. ***True***

F148   Multiple processes share the TLB. ***True***

F149   With larger page size, the page table size will be correspondingly larger. ***False***

F150   A process is never prevented from reading or writing some of its own memory. ***False***

F151   It is always the case that every page of a process is brought into main memory (at some point) during the execution of a process. ***False***

F152   A process is always permitted to read or write some of its own memory. ***False***

F153   When the bit in a page table entry is set to 'valid', this value indicates that the associated page is both legal and in memory. ***True***

F154   If a page is valid but not in memory, the valid/invalid bit in the page table entry would be set to 'valid'. ***False***

F155   The *offset* in the logical address must always be less than the *limit* field of the segment table entry. ***True***

F156   An *offset* in the logical address which is greater than the *limit* field of the segment table entry generates a page fault. ***False***

F157   The most frequently used page always causes the most number of page faults. ***False***

F158   The most frequently used page always causes the least number of page faults. ***False***

F159   The least frequently used page always causes the most number of page faults. **_False_**

F160   The least frequently used page always causes the least number of page faults. **_False_**

F161   In general, virtual memory decreases the degree of multiprogramming in a system. **_False_**

F162   A process with too many frames will likely have a high page-fault rate. **_False_**

F163   A page selected for replacement needs to be *always* written to disk. **_False_**

F164   Prepaging reduces the initial page fault rates. **_True_**

F165   Implementation of associative memory requires hardware support. **_True_**

F166   Increasing the TLB reach by increasing the TLB size is expensive (due to high associate memory cost). **_True_**

F167   Increasing TLB reach by increasing the page size is not a common practical approach. **_False_**

F168   The virtual memory can be (theoretically) as large as the secondary (disk) memory size. **_True_**

F169   Increasing the number of entries in the TLB increases the TLB reach. **_True_**

F170   Increasing the page size will not increase the TLB reach. **_False_**.

F171   A process with more pages will always experience more page faults than one with lesser pages. **_False_**

F172   The number of page faults experienced by a process is independent of its access patterns of instructions and data. **_True_**

F173   A thread always blocks on a TLB miss. **_False_**

F174   A thread may continue to run on a TLB miss. **_True_**

F175   Checking for the read / write privileges while accessing a page is (usually) done in hardware. ***True***

F176   There is one inverted page table entry for every logical page. ***False***

F177   There are as many inverted page table entries as there are physical frames. ***True***

F178   The search time in an inverted page table is less than that of a normal page table. ***False***

F179   In a *hashed* page table, no two page numbers can ever hash to the same entry. ***False***

F180   The TLB contains only a subset of the page table entries. ***True***

F181   A page number which is not found in the TLB always results in page fault. ***False***

F182   The physical address space of a process has to be contiguous. ***False***

F183   A process being swapped in has to be brought to the same memory frames it occupied before being swapped out. ***False***

F184   The fundamental working of *paging* is dependent on temporal and spatial locality of programs. ***True***

F185   The fundamental working of *cache* is not dependent on temporal and spatial locality of programs. ***False***

F186   Each entry in the page table contains a bit that indicates if the virtual page is actually mapped to a physical frame. ***True***

F187   All the locations in an associative memory can be looked up in constant time. ***True***

F188   Separate caches are always needed for instructions and data. ***False***

F189   The *first-fit* memory allocation method results in the least fragmentation. ***False***

F190   Segmented memory allocation will not have internal fragmentation. ***True***

F191   The unit of transfer between cache and main memory must equal a word or an addressable unit. ***False***

F192   Each page table entry contains the (logical) page number in addition to the (physical) frame number. ***False***

F193   The K–way set-associate mapping refers to having K sets of cache lines. ***False***

F194   Cache line size could be different from the main memory block size. ***False***

F195   There is a 1:1 correspondence between the number of TLB entries and the number of page table entries. ***False***

F196   Hashed page tables are particularly useful for processes with sparse address spaces. ***True***

F197   Inverted page tables require each process to have its own page table. ***False***

F198   Each entry of the TLB contains the (logical) page number and the corresponding (physical) frame number. ***True***

F199   The number of entries in a TLB depends on the number of pages. ***False***

F200   The TLB entries are sorted by the virtual page numbers. ***False***

F201   In a TLB all the entries need to be searched sequentially. ***False***

F202   Reducing the page size results in increase in the number of TLB entries. ***True***

F203   The page table can also be swapped out to disk occasionally. ***True***

F204   The inverted page table saves space compared to a normal page table. ***True***

F205   Segmentation has fixed-sized blocks. ***False***

F206   Page table entry contains both the page number and the frame number. ***False***

F207   TLB entry does not contain the logical page number. ***False***

F208   In a direct–mapped cache, the cache replacement algorithms are not applicable. ***True***

F209   The order of bytes (or words) in a main memory block and those in the corresponding cache line are the same. ***True***

F210   A process can modify its own address translation table(s). ***False***

F211   The byte offset for an object in physical frame need not be the same as the byte offset in the corresponding logical page. ***False***

F212   Parts of logical memory space of a process may be occupied by the some pages of the operating system. ***True***

F213   In the partition scheme of memory allocation, the size of each process must be less than the physical memory size. ***True***

F214   A TLB hit for a page access guarantees no page fault (for that access). ***True***

F215   The *first-fit* memory allocation method suffers from external fragmentation. ***True***

F216   The *best-fit* memory allocation method does not suffer from external fragmentation. ***False***

F217   The TLB helps in reducing the access to page tables during address translation. ***True***

F218   The TLB entries are searched sequentially. ***False***

F219   The number of TLB entries will be equal to the number of pages in a process. ***False***

F220   There will be one system-wide TLB. ***False***

F221   A multilevel page table reduces the size of page table (compared to single-level page table). ***True***

F222   A multilevel page table reduces the number of page faults (compared to single-level page table). *__False__*

F223   Page table is looked up only after a TLB miss. *__True__*

F224   Memory protection is usually done by the processor and associated hardware. *__True__*

F225   A segment table must always fit within a page. *__False__*

F226   Page fault rate has no effect on effective memory access time. *__False__*

F227   Cache hit ratio has an effect on effective memory access time. *__True__*

F228   The hash values in the entries of a hashed page table correspond to (physical) frame numbers. *__False__*

F229   The FIFO page replacement algorithm could suffer from *Belady's* anomaly. *__True__*

F230   All reference strings (access patterns) using FIFO exhibit *Belady's* anomaly. *__False__*

F231   The *second-chance* algorithm does not suffer from *Belady's* anomaly. *__False__*

F232   Stack algorithms can never exhibit *Belady's* anomaly. *__True__*

F233   Least recently used (LRU) page replacement algorithm does not suffer from *Belady's* anomaly. *__True__*

F234   Distributing heavily used pages evenly over all of memory would reduce page faults. *__True__*

F235   Memory protection is not needed in a single user system. *__False__*

F236   In paged memory systems, increase of page size reduces the internal fragmentation. *__False__*

F237   Page fault cannot occur while trying to store (write) data in memory (RAM). *__False__*

F238   The FIFO page replacement algorithm is the one implemented on most systems. *False*

F239   Any instruction or data access really requires two memory (RAM) accesses. *True*

F240   A process cannot have more than one working set. *False*

F241   A program having good locality of reference would have less page faults. *True*

F242   In a system supporting virtual memory, portions of multiple programs may reside in memory at the same time. *True*

F243   Demand paging works on the principle that only portions of a program are needed / are active in a short time window. *True*

F244   There is no requirement of minimum number of page frames that must be allocated to a running process in a virtual memory environment. *False*

F245   Every page selected to be swapped out need not be written onto disk. *True*

F246   CPU generates physical address (of RAM) during execution. *False*

F247   It is *never* the case that the same (logical) page number of two different processes in the system map to the same (physical) frame number. *False*

F248   Cache data transfers are done in blocks. *True*

F249   Under-allocation of pages for processes causes trashing. *True*

F250   Trashing has no effect on CPU utilization. *False*

F251   Increasing the degree of multiprogramming could reduce trashing. *False*

F252   The CPU generates physical memory (RAM) addresses when executing instructions of a process. *False*

F253   CPU accessing a data item in a page which is not in any memory frame (RAM) causes an interrupt. *__False__*

F254   When significant time is spent in paging, decreasing the degree of multiprogramming improves the CPU utilization. *__True__*

G. I/O subsystem

G1   Spooling facilitates overlapping of I/O and CPU operations. ***True***

G2   An interrupt is a hardware-generated event. ***True***

G3   During DMA data transfer, the CPU just waits for the I/O to complete. ***False***

G4   Using DMA, the data transfer between memory and I/O device, and CPU execution can proceed simultaneously. ***True***

G5   There is one common queue for all devices in a system. ***False***

G6   Direct Memory Access (DMA) is not suitable for slow (ex. keyboard, mouse) devices. ***True***

G7   Direct Memory Access (DMA) is used for any I/O device. ***False***

G8   Direct Memory Access (DMA) is suitable for high speed devices doing bulk data transfers. ***True***

G9   Use of memory-mapped I/O to device control registers eliminates the need for special I/O instructions. ***True***

G10   In memory-mapped I/O, user programs can access memory addresses associated with the device control registers. ***False***

G11   Buffering is not needed with mouse devices. ***False***

G12   Interrupt-driven I/O is not suitable for mouse input. ***False***

G13   Interrupt-driven I/O is suitable for keyboard input. ***True***

G14   Polling is used only for input devices. ***True***

G15   Polling is not needed in memory-mapped devices. ***True***

G16   Interrupts are not needed in memory-mapped devices. ***True***

G17   Interrupts are used only for data transfers from the device to the memory (input device). ***False***

G18   Non-blocking I/O is better suited to mouse and keyboard input. ***True***

G19   Non-blocking I/O is better suited when the order of I/O arrival from multiple devices is not predetermined. ***True***

G20   Interrupt-driven I/O is less efficient than busy waiting (in terms of CPU utilization). ***False***

G21   When the DMA controller is using the memory bus for data transfer, the CPU waits if it needs to use of the bus. ***True***

G22   Interrupt-driven I/O is more efficient than polling under any circumstance. ***False***

G23   When I/O is frequent and of short duration, polling is efficient. ***True***

G24   I/O operations (typically) take place synchronously with respect to the CPU. ***False***

G25   All kinds of I/O requests by a process will result in the process getting transitioned to waiting state. ***False***

G26   During a DMA I/O transfer, if the CPU wants to do a memory access, the DMA transfer is paused. ***False***

G27   Notification of completion of I/O transfer is done via a trap (exception). ***False***

G28   Memory-mapped I/O can be used only with an interrupt-driven device driver. ***False***

G29   Memory-mapped I/O can be used with a polling-based device driver. ***True***

G30   The I/O module is the interface between the CPU and the peripheral device. ***True***

G31   In programmed I/O, the CPU is tied up during a data transfer from the device to I/O module. ***True***

G32   Drivers are specific to a given operating-system. ***True***

G33   CPU is actively involved in DMA mode data transfer. ***False***

G34   In DMA transfer, an interrupt is generated for every byte of transfer. ***False***

G35   The CPU has to continuously monitor the DMA I/O transfers. ***False***

G36   The device controller communicates directly with the operating system. ***False***

G37   Direct memory access (DMA) is not suitable for all devices. ***True***

G38   Some devices combine both polling and interrupts. ***True***

G39   In *polling*, the CPU must periodically scan (read) an address to check if an input has arrived. ***True***

G40   The CPU will be waiting while the DMA systems transfers data between memory and I/O device. ***False***

G41   In busy wait mode of I/O, the CPU will be waiting for I/O to complete. ***True***

G42   Interrupts are due to events that occur outside of processor execution. ***True***

G43   Every keyboard click may not cause an interrupt. ***False***

G44   A device completing an I/O operation generates a trap. ***False***

G45   There are different drivers for a given device for different operating systems. ***True***

G46   For CPUs having explicit I/O instructions, I/O protection can also be ensured by executing the I/O instructions in user mode. ***False***

G47   When I/O is frequent and of short duration interrupt-driven I/O is not efficient. ***True***

H. Secondary (disk) storage and file system

H1   Higher speed disk drives (compared to lower speed ones) do not necessarily improve the rotational latency. ***False***

H2   In general, LOOK disk head scheduling will involve less movement of the disk heads than SCAN disk head scheduling. ***True***

H3   The outer track of platter in a disk drive has more sectors than the inner track(s). ***False***

H4   All the sectors on a given track are not of the same size. ***False***

H5   The sectors on different tracks of a magnetic disk are of the same (physical) size. ***False***

H6   Every sector, irrespective of the track, contains the same amount of data. ***True***

H7   Rotational delay (search time) is the slowest of the three components of disk I/O. ***False***

H8   In movable head disk drives, the read/write heads of different platters could be on different tracks. ***False***

H9   In fixed–head disk drives, the seek time is the slowest component of disk I/O. ***False***

H10   The track(s) of platters of magnetic disk drives are spiral. ***False***

H11   Seek time depends on the disk's RPM. ***False***

H12   Rotational latency (delay) is independent of the disk's RPM. ***False***

H13   With constant angular velocity disk drive, the same amount of data is under the head across all tracks. ***True***

H14   With constant angular velocity disk drive, the storage density decreases going from outside to inside. ***False***

H15   With constant angular velocity disk drive, the number of sectors on each track decreases going from outside to inside. **_False_**

H16   In constant linear velocity disk drive, the density of tracks increases going from outer tracks to inner tracks. **_False_**

H17   In constant linear velocity disk drive, the density of tracks is the same across tracks. **_True_**

H18   All files in a single-level directory must have unique names. **_True_**

H19   A relative path name must begin at the root. **_False_**

H20   An absolute path name must always begin at the root. **_True_**

H21   SSTF disk scheduling algorithm may cause starvation of some requests. **_True_**

H22   In C-SCAN algorithm, the arm moves in only one direction while servicing requests. **_True_**

H23   The seek time of a disk drive is dependent on the rotation speed. **_False_**

H24   The SSTF disk head scheduling algorithm does not take into account the current position of the disk head. **_False_**

H25   The SCAN disk head scheduling algorithm does not take into account the current position of the disk head. **_True_**

H26   Polling is inefficient for devices with unpredictable I/O operations. **_True_**

H27   Interrupt has relatively low overhead compared to polling. **_False_**

H28   DMA I/O operation delivers data directly to the memory of a process. **_False_**

H29   A large fraction of the I/O software in an operating system is device dependent. **_False_**

H30   The device driver has reentrant code. **_True_**

H31   SCAN and C-SCAN disk scheduling algorithms could lead to starvation of request(s). **_True_**

H32   The disk block allocation methods have no influence on the performance of disk scheduling algorithms. **_False_**

H33   Disk controllers do not usually have a built-in cache. **_False_**

H34   Tertiary storage is usually implemented as a jukebox of tapes or removable disks. **_True_**

H35   The LOOK disk head scheduling offers no practical benefit over SCAN disk head scheduling. **_False_**

H36   The LOOK disk head scheduling involves (in general) less movement of the disk heads than SCAN scheduling. **_True_**

H37   RAID Level 1 organization achieves better performance for read requests. **_True_**

H38   There is more overhead for the write operations on a RAID Level 5 system compared to RAID Level 1 organization. **_True_**

H39   The throughput in the RAID system is independent of the number of disks. **_False_**

H40   The disk scheduling algorithms could only manage the reduction of seek time. **_True_**

H41   The rotational latency is higher than the seek time. **_False_**

H42   In contiguous allocation, the disk head movement is minimized. **_True_**

H43   Linked allocation of file supports direct access efficiently. **_False_**

H44   Indexed allocation of file supports direct access efficiently. **_True_**

H45   Disk fragmentation is avoided in linked allocation of files. **_True_**

H46   Disk fragmentation exists in indexed allocation of files. **_False_**

H47   Error detection is used in RAID level 0. **_False_**

H48   RAID 0 does not use parity bits. ***True***

H49   In RAID, a few large-capacity disk drives are preferable to several small-capacity disk drives. ***False***

H50   In RAID, the data distributed across multiple disks cannot be simultaneously accessed. ***False***

H51   RAID level 2 provides error correction of bytes. ***True***

H52   RAID level 3 provides only error detection, but not error correction of sectors. ***False***

H53   A separate disk for parity of the blocks of other disks is used in RAID level 5. ***False***

H54   The parity of the blocks of the disks is spread across all the disks in RAID level 4. ***False***

H55   The failure of a disk can never be recovered in any RAID level. ***False***

H56   Potential overuse of the single parity disk can occur with RAID level 4. ***True***

H57   Only error detection, but not error correction is supported in RAID level 6. ***False***

IOIOIOIOIOIOIOIOIOIOIOIOIOIOIOIOIOIOIOIOIOIOIOIOIOIOIOIOIOI

Answers

(Sentence Completion)

A. Introduction and OS structure

A1   User programs make use of Operating System services by the use of ***system calls***.

A2   ***Multiprogramming*** refers to multiple programs in various states of execution to be in the memory at the same time.

A3   The privileged instructions are executed in ***kernel (supervisory/privileged)*** mode.

A4   ***Bootloader*** stored in ROM starts up first when the machine is powered on.

A5   ***Microkernel*** is the bare essential kernel in which the nonessential components have been implemented as user programs.

A6   The (small) code that locates the kernel and loads it into main memory (RAM) is called ***bootloader***.

A7   A program that has been invoked (started) is called a ***process***.

A8   The most common secondary storage device is ***magnetic disk***.

A9   A ***timer*** can be used to prevent a user program from never returning control to the operating system.

A10   Embedded systems typically employ a ***real-time*** operating system.

A11   The servers may sometimes act as clients in a ***peer-to-peer system***.

A12   Two important design issues for cache memory are ***cache size*** and ***replacement policy***.

A13   The bootstrap program is stored on ***ROM*** (or ***EEPROM***).

A14   A ***linkage editor (linker)*** combines multiple object modules into a single binary.

A15   The core (essential) part of the OS which interacts with the hardware is the ***kernel***.

A16   More memory required (dynamically) by a running process is allocated on the ***heap*** area of memory.

A17   The notion of operating system supporting than one runnable program to be in memory is called ***multiprogramming***.

A18   User programs can invoke functions in the operating system kernel by the use of ***system calls***.

A19   The notion of operating system supporting than one user is called ***multiuser OS***.

A20   Turning off (disabling) interrupts can only be done in ***kernel (supervisory)*** mode.

A21   Use of separate partitions of a single system to support a different operating systems is called ***virtualization***.

A22   A specialized computer system that is part of a larger physical system is called ***embedded system.***

A23   The bootstrap loader stored on ROM is also referred to as ***firmware***.

A24   The primary part of the operating system that performs the system's most essential tasks is called the ***kernel***.

A25   The first (small) program to run when a computer system is powered on is the ***bootstrap loader***.

A26   The bootstrap loader is resident in ***ROM*** or ***EEPROM***.

A27   When the bootstrap loader runs, it loads the ***kernel*** from ***disk*** onto ***main memory (RAM)***.

A28   Instructions of the user programs run in ***user*** mode.

A29   Instructions of the OS functions run in ***kernel*** mode.

A30   The kernel mode is also called ***supervisor mode*** or ***privileged mode***.

A31   The mode of execution (user or kernel) is indicated by ***a hardware bit***.

A32   The address of the next instruction to be executed is contained in the **_program counter_**.

A33   Multiple OS environments existing simultaneously on the same machine, isolated from each other is called **_virtual machine_**.

A34   The three major queues on a typical system are **_ready_**, **_run_**, and **_I/O_**.

A35   I/O-bound processes typically have **_short_** CPU bursts.

A36   Routines that are never used are never loaded when using **_dynamic_** loading.

A37   The tiny bootstrap loader program stored in the **_ROM_** (or **_EEPROM_**) brings the full bootstrap program from the **_disk_**.

A38   Two primary models of interprocess communication are **_shared memory_** and **_message passing._**

A39   **_Shared memory_** model is better suited for communication between processors within a multiprocessor system.

A40   A kernel that is stripped of all nonessential components is called **_microkernel_**.

A41   A **_full bootstrap loader_** loads the operating system and begin its execution.

A42   Interface to the operating system services are available to user programs via **_system calls_**.

A43   A table of pointers to interrupt-service routines is called **_interrupt vector_**.

A44   An interrupt is handled by a(n) **_interrupt service routine_ (or _interrupt handler)_**.

A45   A trap is handled by a(n) **_system call_**.

A46   The list of starting addresses of the interrupt service routines is contained in **_interrupt vector_**.

A47   User programs make use of Operating System services by the use of ***system calls***.

A48   Attempt to access a memory location by a user process which has no permission, generates a ***trap***.

A49   The preferred method of process communication in a distributed system is ***message passing***.

A50   Common methods used to pass parameters to the operating system during system calls are via ***registers***, ***a block of memory***, or ***stack***.

A51   In multiprocessor environments, ensuring multiple caches store the most recent version of data is called ***cache coherency***.

A52   Interrupts are handled (processed) in ***kernel*** mode.

A53   The full bootstrap program is stored at a fixed location on the disk (partition) called the ***boot blocks***.

A54   A software interrupt caused by an event internal to a process is called ***trap***.

A55   Before starting the interrupt service routine (ISR), interrupts are ***disabled***.

A56   After finishing the interrupt service routine (ISR), interrupts are ***enabled***.

A57   Modifying entries in device-status table must be done in ***kernel (supervisory)*** mode.

A58   An interrupt caused by software is called ***trap (or exception)***.

A59   Accessing a NULL pointer causes a ***trap (or exception)***.

A60   The major resources managed by the operating system are: ***CPU, memory, files, I/O devices***.

A61   ***Interrupt*** is based on conditions occurring outside the processor.

A62   ***Exception*** is based on conditions occurring within the processor.

A63   The earliest the service of an interrupt can be started is ___after the completion of the current instruction___.

A64   During program execution, a divide by zero causes a(n) ___trap (or exception)___.

A65   The main advantage of implementing operating systems in a high-level language is ___portability___.

A66   A computing system used in time-critical environments is called a ___real-time system___.

A67   Absolute code can be generated for ___compile-time___ binding.

A68   The mechanism that links applications to libraries at run time is called ___dynamic linking___.

A69   The initialization of the CPU registers, device controllers, and memory is done by ___boot-strap loader___.

A70   In multithreaded programs, the kernel informs an application about certain events, using a procedure known as a(n) ___upcall___.

A71   The state of an interrupted process is stored in ___the process control block (PCB)___.

A72   The entries of all the process control blocks (PCBs) of the current processes is in ___process table___.

A73   The context switch happening due to a process initiating ___an I/O operation___ is considered voluntary.

A74   The correct sequence of actions when an interrupt occurs, among the following actions: (a) save the context of the current task in its TCB; (b) execute the ISR; (c) disable further interrupts; (d) complete the instruction that is currently being executed; (e) return to the interrupted task and continue to execute from where it left off; (f) lookup the interrupt vector to get the address of the interrupt service routine (ISR); are ___(d) – (a) – (c) – (f) –(b) – (e)___.

A75   Attempt to execute an illegal instruction generates an ___exception (or trap)___.

A76　The degree of multiprogramming can be increased if the CPU utilization is ___low___ and the disk utilization is ___low___.

A77　A ___timer___ ensures that a user program always returns control to the operating system.

B. Processes and threads

B1   A **_pipe_** acts as a conduit for two processes to communicate.

B2   A **_socket_** is an end point of communication.

B3   When a running process requests an I/O operation, the scheduler puts it in **_waiting_** state.

B4   After an I/O of a process is completed, it goes to the **_ready_** state.

B5   Taking out a running process and bringing in another process to run is called **_context switch_**.

B6   The essential information of a process required by the OS is stored in the **_process control block (PCB)_**.

B7   **_Ready queue_** contains the list of processes waiting for the CPU.

B8   The number of processes completed per time unit is referred to as **_throughput_**.

B9   A process can go to the _running_ state only from **_ready_** state.

B10   A process can go to the _terminated_ state only from **_running_** state.

B11   A process can go to the _waiting_ state only from **_running_** state.

B12   A blocking send() and blocking receive() is known as **_rendezvous_**.

B13   APIs for creating and managing threads is provided by **_thread library_**.

B14   The POSIX standard for APIs for thread creation and synchronization is called **_Pthreads_**.

B15   A **_thread pool_** facilitates use of an existing thread instead of creating a new one to complete a task.

B16   The **_many-to-one_** model maps many user-level threads to one kernel thread.

B17 The ***many-to-many*** multithreading model multiplexes many user-level threads to a smaller or equal number of kernel threads.

B18 ***LWP (light weight process)*** is an intermediate data structure placed between user and kernel threads.

B19 The number of threads (of control) in a traditional (or heavyweight) process is **1**.

B20 The time that a process is expected to use the CPU continuously (without I/O) is called ***CPU burst***.

B21 A preempted process goes from ***running*** to ***ready*** state.

B22 A process requesting an I/O operation goes from ***running*** to ***waiting*** state.

B23 The ***one-to-one*** model maps each user-level thread to one kernel thread.

B24 A thread is immediately terminated in response to cancellation request in ***asynchronous cancellation***.

B25 A thread is terminated at an appropriate time in response to cancellation request in ***deferred cancellation***.

B26 ***Priority inheritance*** is a solution to the *priority inversion* problem.

B27 The situation where a high-priority process becomes ready to execute while a low-priority process is executing in its critical region is called ***priority inversion***.

B28 The situation where a low-priority process is holding a shared resource (non-preemptively) which is required by some high-priority process is called ***priority inversion***.

B29 The major components that are not shared across the threads of the same process are ***thread ID***, ***program counter***, ***register set***, and ***heap***.

B30 The major components that are shared across the threads of the same process are ***code***, ***data***, and ***files***.

B31 The creation, scheduling and management of **_kernel_** threads are done by the operating system.

B32 In the *many-to-one* model, thread management is done in **_user_** space.

B33 A child process which terminates without notifying the parent process is called **_zombie_**.

B34 A process that has terminated but has not yet released the resources is said to be in **_zombie_** state.

B35 A child process whose parent process has terminated is called **_orphan_**.

B36 A thread has its own **_program counter_**, **_stack_**, and **_a set of registers_**.

B37 After an I/O event is completed, a process goes to **_ready_** state.

B38 When the time-quantum of an executing process expires, it goes to the **_ready_** state.

B39 The processor could even switch threads between instructions in **_fine-grained_** multithreading.

B40 A thread could continue to execute on a processor until a long-latency event (ex. memory stall) occurs under **_coarse-grained_** multithreading.

B41 The number of process control blocks (PCBs) in a system with N processes is **_N_**.

B42 The essential information pertaining to a process is stored in the OS in the **_process control block (PCB)_**.

B43 Only from **_running_** state can a process go to the *finish* state.

B44 Only from **_running_** state can a process go to the *waiting* state.

B45 When a process executes an I/O instruction, the scheduler moves it from **_running_** state to **_waiting_** state.

B46   A collection of threads created at process startup is called a ***thread pool***.

B47   Allowing a thread to run on only a specific processor is called ***processor affinity***.

B48   A process being moved from one area of memory to another is called ***relocation***.

B49   Code that can be used by two or more processes at the same time, where executable code is shared and the data areas are separate, is called ***reentrant code***.

B50   A program that has been invoked and is in a state of execution is called a ***process***.

B51   The parts of the process that are shared among the threads of the same process are ***code***, ***data***, and ***files***.

B52   Apart from the process, each of the threads have individually for themselves their own ***registers*** and ***stack***.

B53   Saving the state of the currently running process and restoring the state of the next process to run is done at ***context switch***.

B54   Completion of an I/O event transitions the process to ***ready*** state.

B55   Two primary means of inter-process communication are ***shared memory*** and ***message passing***.

B56   Having more than one thread sharing the process address space is called ***multithreading***.

B57   After an I/O event is completed, a process goes to the ***ready*** state.

B58   Multiple threads of a process communicate using ***shared memory***.

B59   The basic categories of threads are ***user*** threads and ***kernel*** threads.

B60   Temporary data such as local variables, function parameters, and return addresses of process are stored in the ***stack***.

B61   Information about the state of a process is contained in ***process control block (PCB)***.

B62   Two registers used to ensure the validity of the addresses of a process are ***base*** and ***limit*** registers.

B63   The termination of all the descendants of a process being terminated is called ***cascading termination***.

B64   A preferred method of communication when processes are in two different machines is ***message passing***.

B65   Creation of several threads at process startup (even though not all of them are required) provides the benefit of ***lower overhead of repeated thread creations***.

B66   The condition that a process is ready to run but is stuck waiting indefinitely for the CPU is called ***starvation***.

B67   Degree of multiprogramming refers to the number of ***processes*** in memory.

B68   ***Reducing*** the degree of multiprogramming could reduce trashing.

C. CPU Scheduling

C1   The part of the OS that chooses processes to run on the CPU is the ***processor (CPU) scheduler***.

C2   The non–preemptive scheduling algorithm that results in the smallest average waiting time is the ***shortest job next (SJN)***.

C3   The ***round robin (RR)*** scheduling algorithm is designed especially for time-sharing systems.

C4   The lowest level of the multilevel feedback queue use the ***first-come first-served (FCFS)*** scheduling.

C5   The processes with short CPU bursts are at a disadvantage in the ***FCFS*** scheduling algorithm.

C6   All processes are treated fairly (equally) in the ***round-robin (RR)*** scheduling algorithm.

C7   Processes with long CPU-bursts suffer starvation in the ***shortest-job next (SJN)*** scheduling algorithm.

C8   Increasing the context-switch frequency tends to ***decrease*** the average response time of processes.

C9   Increasing the context-switch frequency tends to ***increase*** the CPU utilization.

C10   Executing the shortest tasks first ***decreases*** the average turn-around time of processes.

C11   A process may be interrupted in the middle of its execution in ***preemptive*** scheduling.

C12   A process cannot be suspended before finishing its CPU burst in ***non-preemptive*** scheduling.

C13   The two types of bursts that are used in CPU scheduler design are ***CPU burst*** and ***I/O burst***.

C14   The ***CPU (short–term) scheduler*** chooses processes from the ready queue to run on the CPU.

C15   The ***medium–term*** scheduler decides on the swap-out and swap-in of processes.

C16   Predicting the next CPU burst is used in the ***shortest job first (SJF)*** scheduling algorithm.

C17   ***Aging*** is a technique used to overcome starvation in some CPU scheduling.

C18   In multilevel queue scheduling, the ***ready*** queue is partitioned into separate queues.

C19   The context switch overhead increases when the RR time-quantum is ***reduced***.

C20   The ***CPU (short–term)*** scheduler chooses processes from the ready queue to run on the CPU.

C21   The ***medium–term*** scheduler decides on the swap-out and swap-in of processes.

C22   Given a set of processes with known (best estimates) of CPU bursts, the scheduling algorithm that gives a high throughput is ***shortest job next (SJN)***.

C23   In a single CPU system, the ***shortest job next*** scheduling results in the minimum average turnaround time.

C24   In a single CPU system, the ***shortest job next*** scheduling results in the minimum average waiting time.

C25   The selection of processes to be swapped out of memory is done by the ***medium-term*** scheduler.

C26   Selection of the processes to be brought into the ready queue is done by ***long-term*** scheduler.

C27   Selection of the processes to be executed next (allocated CPU) is done by ***short-term*** scheduler.

C28   The selection of processes to be swapped into memory is done by the ***medium-term*** scheduler.

C29   In the multi-level feedback queue system, the most often run scheduler is the ***short-term*** scheduler.

C30   An objective of the process scheduling policy is to ***maximize*** throughput.

C31   An objective of the process scheduling policy is to ***minimize*** response time.

C32   An objective of the process scheduling policy is to ***minimize*** waiting time.

C33   An objective of the process scheduling policy is to ***minimize*** turnaround time.

C34   An objective of the process scheduling policy is to ***maximize*** CPU usage.

C35   With the time-quantum in the *round-robin* (RR) policy being extremely small, each of the processes perceive the processor to be ***slower*** than its actual speed.

C36   ***Round-robin*** scheduling is essentially the pre-emptive version of ***FCFS***.

C37   The module that gives control of the CPU to the process selected by the short-term scheduler is called ***dispatcher***.

C38   The time taken by the dispatcher to stop one process and start another one running is called ***dispatch latency***.

C39   In FCFS scheduling, a process running with a long CPU burst, causing many processes to wait is called ***convoy effect***.

C40   All processes are treated fairly in ***round-robin*** scheduling.

C41   Turn Around Time = ***Completion Time*** minus ***Arrival Time***.

C42   Waiting Time = ***Turn Around Time*** minus ***Execution Time***.

C43   Compute intensive jobs are given ***larger*** quantum of time, which results in ***fewer*** context switches.

C44   In *Little's formula*, λ represents the ***average arrival rate*** for new processes.

C45   The second-chance algorithm is an extension of the FIFO replacement algorithm by the addition of a ***reference bit***.

C46   In a multi-level queue, a job which has spent significant time in the ***lower level*** queue is moved to a ***higher level*** queue.

C47   The number of processes completing their execution per time unit is called ***throughput***.

C48   The time taken by a process from the time it enters the system till the time it finishes execution is called **turnaround time**.

C49   The amount of time a process spends without using the CPU is called ***waiting time***.

C50   Turnaround time is the sum of ***execution time*** and ***waiting time***.

C51   A technique to the solution of indefinite blockage of low-priority jobs in priority scheduling is ***aging***.

C52   Round-robin (RR) scheduling degenerates to first-come-first-served (FCFS) scheduling if the time-quantum is ***too long***.

C53   In RR scheduling with a time-quantum of Q units, and N processes in ready queue, a process (in ready queue) waits no more than **$(N-1)\,Q$ time units**.

C54   In RR scheduling with a time-quantum of Q units, and N processes in ready queue, the average turn-around time of a process requiring T units of execution time (assuming no process goes to waiting state, and the CPU bursts of other processes is $> T$) is **$T + (N-1)\lfloor T/Q \rfloor \cdot Q$**.

C55   ***Starvation*** is a significant problem with priority scheduling algorithms.

C56   Predicting the next CPU burst of processes is needed in ***shortest job next (SJN)*** scheduling.

C57   Each queue has its own scheduling algorithm in ***multilevel queue*** scheduling.

C58   When the CPU scheduler picks a processes to run on the CPU next, it goes from ***ready*** to ***running*** state.

C59   In a system of N processes, $P_1, \dots P_N$, with CPU bursts of $T_1 \dots T_N$, and $T_1 > T_2 > \dots \dots T_N$, the order of arrival of the processes resulting in the *best* average waiting time under FCFS scheduling, is **$P_N, P_{N-1}, \dots P_1$**.

C60   In a system of N processes, $P_1, \dots P_N$, with CPU bursts of $T_1 \dots T_N$, and $T_1 > T_2 > \dots \dots T_N$, the order of arrival of the processes resulting in the *worst* average waiting time under FCFS scheduling, is **$P_1, P_2, \dots P_N$**.

C61   In round robin (RR) scheduling with a quantum of Q units of time, and N processes with CPU bursts of $T_1 \dots T_N$, the condition for every process requiring more than one timeslot to finish, is **$Q \leq MIN\{T_i\}$**.

C62   In round robin (RR) scheduling with a quantum of Q units of time, and N processes with CPU bursts of $T_1 \dots T_N$, the condition for every process requiring no more than one timeslot to finish, is **$Q \geq MAX\{T_i\}$**.

C63   The number of processes in the ready queue in a single CPU system, with a total of N processes, and L of them in the waiting state, is **$N - (L + 1)$**.

C64   The average turnaround time in a system of 10 processes, with the average waiting time is W units, and the average of the CPU burst times is C units, is **$C + W$** units.

C65   Given that N processes $P_1, P_2, \dots P_N$ have arrived in that order at some time, with CPU requirements of $T_1, T_2, \dots T_N$, the *waiting* time of process P_K using FCFS scheduling is **$T_1 + T_2 + \dots + T_{K-1}$**.

C66   Given that N processes $P_1, P_2, \dots P_N$ have arrived in that order at some time, with CPU requirements of $T_1, T_2, \dots T_N$, the *turnaround* time of process P_K using FCFS scheduling is **$T_1 + T_2 + \dots + T_K$**.

C67   In multilevel queue scheduling, a newly entering process is placed in the ***lowest priority*** queue.

C68   In multilevel queue scheduling, a newly entering process is placed in the ***higher priority*** queue (with a smaller time-quantum).

C69   In a system with 4 processes, each with a CPU burst time of 12 units, and round robin scheduling with a time slice of 5 units, the total context switches before all the processes are completed are **11**.

C70   In a system with four processes (which have arrived at the same time) with CPU burst times of 8, 10, 3, 7, using FCFS scheduling, the average waiting time is **11.75**, and average turn–around time is **18.75**.

C71   In a system with four processes (which have arrived at the same time) with CPU burst times of 8, 10, 3, 7, using SJN (shortest job next), the average waiting time is **7.75**, and average turn–around time is **14.75**.

C72   In a system with four processes (which have arrived at the same time) with CPU burst times of 8, 10, 3, 7, using RR scheduling (with a time-quantum of 2 units), the average waiting time is **15.5**, and average turn–around time is **22.5**.

C73   In a system where three processes arrive at times 0, 1, and 3, with CPU bursts of 4, 5, and 3, the average *waiting* time using non–preemptive SJN (Shortest Job Next) scheduling, is **$(0 + (7 - 1) + (4 - 3)) / 3 = 7 / 3 = 2.33$**.

C74   In a system where three processes arrive at times 0, 1, and 3, with CPU bursts of 4, 5, and 3, the average *turn–around* time using non–preemptive SJN (Shortest Job Next) scheduling, is **$(4 + (12 - 1) + (7 - 3)) / 3 = 19 / 3 = 6.33$**.

C75   In a system where three processes arrive at times 0.0, 0.5, and 1.2, with CPU bursts of 4, 5, and 3, the average *waiting* time using non–preemptive SJN (Shortest Job Next) scheduling, is **$(0 + (7 - 0.5) + (4 - 1.2)) / 3 = 9.3 / 3 = 3.1$**.

C76   In a system where three processes arrive at times 0.0, 0.5, and 1.2, with CPU bursts of 4, 5, and 3, the average *turn–around* time using non–preemptive SJN (Shortest Job Next) scheduling, is **$(4 + (12 - 0.5) + (7 - 1.2)) / 3 = 21.3 / 3 = 7.1$**.

C77   In a system with five processes with arrival times of 0, 2, 3, 6, 10 and CPU burst times of 15, 2, 14, 10, 2, using FCFS, the average waiting time is **16.6**, and average turn–around time is **25.2**.

C78   In a system with five processes with arrival times of 0, 2, 3, 6, 10 and CPU burst times of 15, 2, 14, 10, 2, using SJN (shortest job next), the average waiting time is **11.8**, and average turn–around time is **20.4**.

C79   In a system with five processes with arrival times of 0, 2, 3, 6, 10 and CPU burst times of 15, 2, 14, 10, 2, using SRT (shortest remaining time), the average waiting time is **8.4**, and average turn–around time is **17.0**.

C80   In a system with five processes with arrival times of 0, 2, 3, 6, 10 and CPU burst times of 15, 2, 14, 10, 2, using RR (with a time-quantum of 5 units), the average waiting time is **15.6**, and average turn–around time is **24.2**.

C81   In RR scheduling with a time-quantum of 20 mS, and 5 processes in ready queue, the average turn-around time of a process requiring 305 mS of execution time (assuming no process goes to waiting state, and the CPU bursts of other processes is > 305 mS) is **1505 mS**.

C82   In RR scheduling with a time-quantum of 20 mS, and 5 processes in ready queue, the average turn-around time of a process requiring 290 mS of execution time (assuming no process goes to waiting state, and the CPU bursts of other processes is > 290 mS) is **1410 mS**.

C83   In a single CPU system with a total of N processes, W processes waiting for I/O, the number of processes in the ready queue is $\underline{N-(W+1)}$.

C84   In a system where processes issue an I/O operation every 5 milliseconds (on the average), and the context switch overhead is 0.2 milliseconds, the CPU utilization is **96.15% (5 / 5.2 * 100)**.

D. Process synchronization

D1   In a system with N concurrent processes, the number of possible *critical sections* is **N**.

D2   The ***entry*** section is executed just before entering the critical section.

D3   The bulk of the work of a process is done in its ***remainder*** section.

D4   The number of possible values of a ***binary semaphore*** is **2**.

D5   In a concurrent system, the results of computation being indeterminate is called ***race*** condition.

D6   With multiple resources, a ***counting*** semaphore is required.

D7   Binary semaphores are also called ***mutex locks***.

D8   The busy wait of a semaphore is also called ***spinlock***.

D9   The number of basic operations on a semaphore is **2**.

D10   Updates to shared data are done by concurrent processes in their ***critical*** sections.

D11   The two operations on a (binary) semaphore are ***P (wait)*** and ***V (signal)***.

D12   In the `signal(S)` statement, the operation done on the semaphore value is ***add 1*** (or ***increment by 1***).

D13   The value of a counting semaphore with initial value of 10, after 6 ***wait*** operations and 4 ***signal*** operations would be **8**.

D14   In the *producer–consumer* problem, the ***producer*** process has to wait when the buffer is full.

D15   In the *producer–consumer* problem, the ***consumer*** process has to wait when the buffer is empty.

D16   The ***entry*** section precedes the critical section.

D17 The bulk of operations, other than access to shared variables, are done by a process in the ***remainder*** section.

D18 A ***counting*** semaphore is used to synchronize the access to / use of multiple instances of a resource.

D19 In the *Dining Philosophers* problem, the **wait(chopstick[i])** statement represents picking up a chopstick in the physical world.

D20 The number of writers which may concurrently share the database in the *readers-writers* problem is **1**.

D21 The condition where several processes (or threads) try to access and modify the same data concurrently is called ***race condition***.

D22 The condition where outcome of execution depend on the order in which instructions are executed is called ***race condition***.

D23 An instruction or a set of instructions which execute as an uninterruptible unit that that is said to execute ***atomically***.

D24 If operations on semaphores are not done atomically, the ***mutual exclusion*** condition may be violated.

D25 In a system with N cooperating processes, the number of critical sections is **N**.

D26 The number of copies of a semaphore used by N cooperating processes for synchronization is **1**.

D27 The number of philosophers who may eat simultaneously in the *Dining Philosophers* problem with 5 philosophers is **2**.

D28 A process checks if can enter the critical section in the ***entry section***.

D29 ***Waiting queues*** are used to prevent busy waiting when implementing a semaphore.

D30 The data streamed from a Web server to a client fits the ***producer-consumer*** model.

D31 Cooperative clients accessing a database fits the ***readers-writers*** model.

D32   In the classical bounded-buffer problem the number of semaphores is **3**.

D33   In the classical *bounded-buffer* problem the number of binary semaphores is **1** and the number of counting semaphores is **2**.

D34   In the classical *bounded-buffer* problem the counting semaphores indicate the ***number of empty slots*** and ***filled slots in the buffer***.

D35   In the classical *bounded-buffer* problem the purpose of the binary semaphore is ***to control access to the shared buffer (mutual exclusive access to shared buffer)***.

D36   Busy waiting can be prevented when implementing a semaphore by the use of ***waiting queues***.

D37   The bounded-buffer is implemented as a ***circular queue***.

D38   In the bounded-buffer problem, the sum of the number of empty slots and number of occupied slots in the buffer is always equal to the ***buffer size***.

D39   In the readers-writers problem ***writers*** are given exclusive access to shared objects.

D40   A synchronization mechanism that is built into a programming language is ***monitor***.

D41   Two (or more) processes which do not affect each other during execution are called ***independent*** processes.

D42   Requiring a bound on the number of times that other threads are allowed to enter their critical sections after a thread has made a request to enter its critical section avoids ***starvation***.

D43   A ***monitor*** type presents a set of programmer-defined operations that are provided mutual exclusion within it.

D44   In a system with two cooperating processes $P1$ and $P2$ sharing a common variable named **x** with an initial value of 15, and $P1$ doing **x++** and $P2$ doing **x--**, the possible values of **x** (without any synchronization) after $P1$ and $P2$ finish execution, are **14, 15, and 16**.

D45 A process can only access/update shared data in its ***critical section***.

D46 In a system with two cooperating processes, a possible effect of a process calling **signal()** before entering critical section, and **wait()** after exiting critical section would be ***multiple processes to be in their critical sections at the same time***.

D47 Algorithms that avoid mutual exclusion are called ***non-blocking synchronization algorithms***.

D48 Concurrent accesses to ***shared*** data without ***synchronization*** may result in data inconsistency.

D49 The three requirements of a solution to the critical section problem are ***mutual exclusion***, ***progress***, and ***bounded waiting***.

D50 The condition where a process is prevented from execution due to waiting for resources that never become available is called ***starvation***.

D51 The condition where the states of cooperating processes constantly change with regard to one another, but none progresses toward completion is called ***livelock***.

D52 Given that the value of a counting semaphore at some instant is C, and subsequently M **wait** operations and N **signal** operations are done on the semaphore, the resulting value of the semaphore is $\underline{C - M + N}$.

D53 Given the *producer–consumer* problem using a semaphore *mutex* (with an initial value of 1) for mutual exclusive access to the buffer, the value of *mutex* when neither producer nor consumer is in its critical section, is **1**.

D54 Given the *producer–consumer* problem using a semaphore *mutex* (with an initial value of 1) for mutual exclusive access to the buffer, the value of *mutex* when the producer is in its critical section, is **0**.

D55 Given the *producer–consumer* problem using a semaphore *mutex* (with an initial value of 1) for mutual exclusive access to the buffer, the value of *mutex* when the consumer is in its critical section, is **0**.

D56   Executing a loop just waiting for an event (condition) to occur is called ***busy waiting***.

E. Deadlocks

E1   The minimum possible number of jobs required to cause deadlocks is **2**.

E2   The minimum possible number of resources required to cause deadlocks is **2**.

E3   The number of necessary conditions for a deadlock to happen is **4**.

E4   The *minimum* number of victim processes/jobs in order to break deadlock is **1**.

E5   Process P_0 waiting for a resource held by P_1, P_1 waiting for a resource held by P_2, and so on, and P_n waiting for a resource held by P_0 is referred to as ***circular wait***.

E6   Two or more processes waiting indefinitely for an event that can be caused by only one of the other waiting processes is known as a ***deadlock*** condition.

E7   The *Banker's algorithm* is used for ***avoidance*** of deadlocks.

E8   In a *safe* system, with M (L) being the most (least) number of remaining resources (requests) of a job, the system must have at least ***L*** resources.

E9   Deadlock (prevention / avoidance) ***prevention*** is not practical.

E10   Deadlock recovery always requires identifying a ***victim*** process/job to be terminated.

E11   The situation when every process in a set is waiting for an event that can only be caused by another process in the set is called ***deadlock***.

E12   The condition where at least one resource is held in a non-sharable mode is called ***mutual exclusion***.

E13   The condition where a process is holding one resource and waiting to acquire additional resources is called ***hold and wait***.

E14   The condition where a resource can be released only voluntarily by the process holding the resource is called ***non preemption***.

E15   A simple mechanism of deadlock recovery is ***rollback***.

E16   Deadlock state is a subset of ***unsafe*** state.

E17   The minimum number of processes required for a deadlock to occur is **2**.

E18   In a resource-allocation graph, a directed edge from a process to a resource is called a ***request edge***.

E19   In a resource-allocation graph, a directed edge from a resource to a process is called an ***assignment edge***.

E20   In a resource-allocation graph, a directed edge indicating that a process may request a resource at some time in the future is called ***claim edge***.

E21   A situation where the system can allocate resources to each process in some order, and still avoid a deadlock is called ***safe state***.

E22   Presence of a cycle in the ***wait-for*** graph indicates deadlock.

E23   Presence of a cycle in the ***resource-allocation*** graph may not indicate deadlock.

E24   In a system with 15 instances of some resource, and each process requiring 3 instances of the resource, the maximum number of processes for which the system never enters into deadlock is **5**.

E25   In a system with 3 processes sharing resources of the same type, with peak demands of 3, 4 and 6, the minimum number of resources of that type required to ensure that a deadlock will not occur is **6**.

E26   With three resources, R_1, R_2, and R_3, each assigned unique integer values 12, 10, and 15, respectively, the resource ordering which prevents a circular wait is ***R_2, R_1, R_3***.

E27   With three resources, R_1, R_2, and R_3, each assigned unique integer values 18, 20, and 14, respectively, the resource ordering which prevents a circular wait is **R_3, R_1, R_2**.

E28   At some point of time, if L is the minimum of the remaining resources required across all jobs, and A is the available resources in the system, the condition that should hold for the system to be in *safe state* is $A \geq L$

E29   The graph derived from the resource allocation graph by removing the resource nodes and collapsing the appropriate edges is called ***wait-for graph***.

E30   Mechanisms for deadlock handling are provided by the ***operating system***.

E31   The four conditions that must hold simultaneously in a system for a deadlock to occur are ***mutual exclusion***, ***hold and wait***, ***no preemption***, and ***circular wait***.

E32   In a system with one resource type, and 3 user processes whose maximum demands for the resource are 3, 4, and 5, the *minimum* instances of the resource required to ensure that deadlock will never occur, is **10**.

E33   In a system with 3 user processes, each requiring 2 units of resource R, the *minimum* number of units (instances) of R such that no deadlocks will ever arise is **4**.

E34   Given that the instances of a resource needed by processes P_1, P_2, ... P_N are R_1, R_2, ... R_N, respectively, the minimum number of resource instances required to ensure that deadlock will never occur is **$(R_1 - 1) + (R_2 - 1) + ... + (R_N - 1) + 1 = (R_1 + R_2 + ... + R_N) - N + 1$**.

E35   The minimum number of resources (of the same type) which are shared by 3 processes which have peak demands of X, Y, and Z instances of the resource is **$(X - 1) + (Y - 1) + (Z - 1) + 1 = X + Y + Z - 2$**.

E36   Given N processes and each process needing a maximum of M resources (of the same type), the *minimum* number of resources, R to ensure that the system is deadlock free, is **$R \geq N(M - 1) + 1$**.

E37   The condition that always holds (invariant) between the sum of the elements of a column j of the *allocation matrix C*, the jth elements of the *existence vector E*, and the *available vector A*, is **$C_j\text{-sum} + A_j = E_j$**

E38   Given that C_K is the sum of the values of the Kth column of the current allocation matrix, the relationship between the Kth element of existence vector E, the Kth element of available vector A, and C_K is **$E_K = C_K + A_K$**

E39   Given that there are N nodes in the resource graph, and the time taken (on the average) to detect a cycle is T, the *best case* time for detecting a deadlock is **T**. (Cycle detected by the cycle detection algorithm on the first node chosen)

E40   Given that there are N nodes in the resource graph, and the time taken (on the average) to detect a cycle is T, the *worst case* time for detecting a deadlock is **NT**. (Cycle is detected when processing the last node or cycle is not detected)

E41   In a system with 12 instances of a resource and 3 processes, and given the maximum resource needs of 5, 8, 7, and current allocations of 3, 5, 4, respectively, the system is in ***deadlock*** state.

E42   In a system with 12 instances of a resource and 3 processes, and given the maximum resource needs of 10, 3, 7, and current allocations of 4, 2, 4, respectively, the system is in ***safe*** state.

E43   In a system with 12 instances of a resource and 3 processes, and given the maximum resource needs of 6, 4, 7, and current allocations of 5, 2, 4, respectively, the system is in ***safe*** state.

E44   In a system with 10 instances of a resource and 3 processes, and given the maximum resource needs of 10, 5, 8, and current allocations of 4, 4, 1, respectively, the system is in ***unsafe*** state.

E45   In a system with 14 instances of a resource and 4 processes, and given the maximum resource needs of 5, 8, 7, 3, and current allocations of 3, 5, 4, 1, respectively, the system is in ***deadlock*** state.

E46   In a system with 14 instances of a resource and 4 processes, and given the maximum resource needs of 4, 6, 5, 9, and current allocations of 1, 4, 0, 8, respectively, the system is in ***safe*** state.

E47   In a system with 10 instances of a resource and 3 processes, and given the maximum resource needs of 10, 3, 6, and current allocations of 4, 1, 4, respectively, the system is in ***deadlock*** state.

E48   In a system with 10 instances of a resource and 3 processes, and given the maximum resource needs of 10, 3, 6, and current allocations of 6, 2, 1, respectively, the system is in ***unsafe*** state.

E49   In a system with 12 instances of a resource and 3 processes, and given the maximum resource needs of 10, 4, 7, and current allocations of 4, 2, 4, respectively, the system is in ***safe*** state.

E50   In a system with 10 instances of a resource and 3 processes, and given the maximum resource needs of 8, 2, 6, and a set of current allocations which would result in the system being in *unsafe* state is **5, 1, 3**.

E51   In a system with 12 instances of a resource and 3 processes, and given the maximum resource needs of 12, 4, 7, and a set of current allocations which would result in the system being in *unsafe* state is **6, 2, 2**.

E52   Given a system with ({allocated}; {waiting-for}) tuples for three process to be P1: (R2; None), P2: (R1; R3), and P3: (R3; R2), the system is (deadlocked / not deadlocked) ***not deadlocked***.

E53   Given a system with ({allocated}; {waiting-for}) tuples for three process to be P1: (R2; R1), P2: (R1; R3), and P3: (R3; R2), the system is (deadlocked / not deadlocked) ***deadlocked***. (circular wait)

E54   Given a system with ({allocated}; {waiting-for}) tuples for three process to be P1: (R1; R3), P2: (R3; R1), and P3: (R2; None), the system is (deadlocked / not deadlocked) ***deadlocked***. (P1 is holding R1 which P2 needs, and P2 is holding R3 which P1 needs)

E55   Given a system with ({allocated}; {waiting-for}) tuples for three process to be P1: (R2; None), P2: (R3; R1), and P3: (R1; R2), the system is (deadlocked / not deadlocked) ***not deadlocked***.

E56   Given a system with ({allocated}; {waiting-for}) tuples for three process to be P1: (R3; None), P2: (R2; R1), and P3: (R1; R2), the system is (deadlocked / not deadlocked) ***deadlocked***.

E57   Given a system with ({allocated}; {waiting-for}) tuples for three process to be P1: (R2, R3; None), P2: (None; R1), and P3: (R1; R2), the system is (deadlocked / not deadlocked) ***not deadlocked***.

E58   Given a system consisting of M resources of the same type shared by N processes, with resources requested and released by processes only one at a time, for the system to be deadlock free, the maximum need of each process is between **1** and **M** resources.

E59   Given a system consisting of M resources of the same type shared by N processes, with resources requested and released by processes only one at a time, for the system to be deadlock free, the sum of all maximum needs is less than **$M + N$**.

E60   The difference of the vectors E (resources in existence) and A (resources available) represents ***the number of resources allocated***.

E61   In the *banker's* algorithm the vector of length M, where M is the number of resource types, denotes the ***availability*** of the resources.

E62   In a system with N processes and M resource types, the ***allocation*** matrix in the *banker's* algorithm denotes the resources allocated to processes.

E63   In a system with N processes and M resource types, the *max* matrix in the *banker's* algorithm denotes the ***maximum needs of resources*** of the processes.

E64   In a system with N processes and M resource types, the *need* matrix in the *banker's* algorithm is obtained by subtracting the ***allocation*** matrix from the ***max*** matrix.

E65   In a system with N instances of a single resource, out of which M $(< N)$ of the resource instances have been allocated, the condition to be satisfied by the resource need Q of any process P_i such that the system will be in a safe state, is $Q \le N - M$.

E66   Given 12 processes sharing 17 instances of a resource, which are reserved and released one at a time, and a sufficient condition for T_R, the sum of the maximum resource needs of all processes to ensure no deadlock, is ***$T_R < 17 + 12$***.

E67   Given a system with resource types R1 and R2, each with two instances, and 4 processes with corresponding ({requested}; {allocated}) tuples to be P1: (R1; R2), P2: (– ; R1), P3: (R2; R1), P4: (– ; R2), the resource allocation graph (does/does not) **_does_** have a cycle, and (is/ is not) **_is not_** deadlocked.

E68   Given a system with resource types R1 and R2, each with two instances, and 4 processes with corresponding ({requested}; {allocated}) tuples to be P1: (R1; R2), P2: (R2 ; R1), P3: (R2; R1), P4: (– ; R2), the resource allocation graph (does/does not) **_does_** have a cycle, and (is/ is not) **_is not_** deadlocked.

E69   Given a system with two types of resources, R1 and R2, each with two instances, and four processes with corresponding ({requested}; {allocated}) tuples to be P1: (R1; R2), P2: (R2 ; R1), P3: (R2; R1), P4: (R1 ; R2), the resource allocation graph (does/does not) **_does_** have a cycle, and (is / is not) **_is_** deadlocked.

E70   Given a system with three types of resources, R1, R2, and R3, with one, two, and one instances, respectively, and three processes with corresponding ({requested}; {allocated}) tuples to be P1: (R1; R2), P2: (R3; {R1, R2}), P3: (R2; R3), the resource allocation graph (does/does not) **_does_** have a cycle, and (is / is not) **_is_** deadlocked.

E71   Given a system has 12 instances of a resource, and 3 processes with their respective (*maximum need, currently owned*) tuples to be (10, 4), (3, 2), and (7, 4), the state of the system is in **_safe_** state.

F. Memory management and virtual memory

F1   The hardware unit that maps logical (virtual) addresses to physical addresses is the ***memory management unit (MMU)***.

F2   The ***valid bit*** in the page table indicates whether the page is in a physical frame or not.

F3   A reference to a page that is not in main memory results in ***page fault***.

F4   The ***inverted page table*** is indexed by the physical frame number and the entries are page numbers.

F5   The number of entries in the TLB multiplied by the page size is the ***TLB reach***.

F6   The page table entry contains the ***physical frame number***.

F7   The contents of the entries in a TLB are ***page number*** and ***frame number***.

F8   The contents of the entries in segment table are ***limit*** and ***base***.

F9   The ***use (dirty)*** bit is useful when a page is selected for replacement.

F10   The ***PTBR (page table base register)*** contains the starting address of the page table in memory.

F11   In a TLB, all the entries are searched simultaneously using ***associative memory*** technology.

F12   A page fault causes a ***trap*** to the operating system.

F13   When the CPU generates a logical address (for instruction or data), its corresponding page number is first looked up in the ***translation look-aside buffer (TLB)***.

F14   The addresses generated by the CPU are ***logical*** addresses.

F15   The addresses generated by the memory management unit (MMU) are *__physical__* addresses.

F16   In a *hashed* page table, the entries are the hash values of *__(virtual)__* *__page numbers__*.

F17   Paging has *__internal__* fragmentation.

F18   *__Segmentation__* has external fragmentation.

F19   A running process requesting more memory (dynamically) may not result in relocation of the entire process under *__pure paging scheme__* (memory allocation).

F20   Translation of virtual addresses to physical addresses under segmentation requires *__base__* register and *__extent__* register.

F21   By paging the segments, wasted memory due to *__external fragmentation__* is reduced.

F22   When a program occupies only a small portion of its large virtual address space, the preferred address mapping is the use of *__a hashed page table__*.

F23   Contiguous memory allocation scheme suffers from *__external__* fragmentation.

F24   Pure segmentation scheme suffers from *__external__* fragmentation.

F25   Paging suffers from *__internal__* fragmentation.

F26   The actual starting address of a job/process in main memory is stored in the *__relocation__* register.

F27   For each active job, the size of the job and the memory location where the page table is stored is in the *__job table__*.

F28   In a page size of 512 bytes, the *maximum* possible unused bytes is __511__.

F29   In a page size of 2048 bytes, the *minimum* possible unused bytes is __0__.

F30   In a system with N processes, the number of page tables (page map tables) is ___N___.

F31   Given that a process of N pages accesses K ($\leq N$) distinct pages during its execution, the minimum number of page faults is ___K___.

F32   The main memory frame numbers corresponding to the logical page numbers of a process is contained in the ***page table (or page map table)***.

F33   A page selected for swapping out is not written on disk if the ***modified (or dirty)*** bit is not set.

F34   With increase of cache access time, the average memory access time ***increases***.

F35   With increase in TLB size, the average memory access time ***decreases***.

F36   The entries of a translation look-aside buffer (TLB) are implemented as ***associative memory***.

F37   Each entry in an Inverted Page Table contains a pair ***process ID*** and ***(logical) page number***.

F38   The page needed at the farthest point in the future is the candidate for replacement in the ***Optimal (OPT)*** page replacement algorithm.

F39   The page referenced at the farthest point in the past is the candidate for replacement in the ***Least Recently Used (LRU)*** page replacement algorithm.

F40   The set of pages used by some number of most recent memory references is called ***working set***.

F41   The ***working set*** is an approximation of a program's locality.

F42   Only a fraction of a process's ***working set*** needs to be stored in the TLB.

F43   Cache works on the principle of ***locality of references***.

F44   The single cache where instructions and data stored is called ***unified cache***.

F45   A currently referenced memory location being highly likely to be referenced again in the near future is called ***temporal locality***.

F46   Accessing a given set of memory locations repetitively over a short period of time is called ***temporal locality***.

F47   The high likelihood of references to memory locations in the near future which are closer to currently referenced locations is called ***spatial locality***.

F48   Accessing a given set of memory locations repetitively, which are in close physical proximity (memory addresses) is called ***spatial locality***.

F49   The *minimum* internal fragmentation in a system with a page size of P bytes, is **0**.

F50   The *maximum* internal fragmentation in a system with a page size of P bytes, is ***P − 1***.

F51   An address generated by a CPU is referred to as ***logical address***.

F52   The mapping of a logical address to a physical address is done in hardware by the ***memory-management-unit (MMU)***.

F53   With segmentation, a logical address consists of ***segment number*** and ***offset***.

F54   The starting address of the page table in memory is contained in the ***Page Table Base Register (PTBR)***.

F55   There is a *valid-invalid* bit for every ***page table entry***.

F56   The separation of physical memory and logical memory is provided by the concept of ***virtual memory***.

F57   A cache ***miss*** refers to the case when a CPU reference cannot be found in cache.

F58   The simplest mapping technique which maps each block of main memory into only one possible cache line is called ***direct mapping***.

F59   The ***tag*** bits are used to determine which memory block is resident in a cache line.

F60   The mapping where any main memory block can be mapped to any cache line is called ***(fully) associative***.

F61   The technique (mode) where all write operations made to main memory are immediately made to the cache as well is called ***write through***.

F62   The technique (mode) where all write operations made to main memory are written to the cache at a later time is called ***write back***.

F63   The ***split*** cache design eliminates contention for the cache between the instruction fetch/decode unit and the execution unit.

F64   Wasted space within a partition is called ***internal fragmentation***.

F65   Page numbers are given by ***higher*** order bits of the logical address.

F66   Offsets within a page are given by ***lower*** order bits of the logical address.

F67   Variable size segments are further divided into fixed size pages in the ***segmented paging*** scheme.

F68   During page replacement, selection of the victim from among the pages of the same process is called ***local replacement***.

F69   During page replacement, selection of the victim page from among the pages of any process is called ***global replacement***.

F70   On a TLB miss, the operating system accesses the ***page table***.

F71   In ***demand*** paging, a page is brought into memory only when it is accessed / needed.

F72   The byte offset in memory frame with respect to the byte offset in the corresponding page is (larger / the same / smaller) ***the same***.

F73   The mapping information of logical pages to main memory frames is contained in *__page table__*.

F74   The *__status__* field in the page table indicates whether the page is in a memory frame or not.

F75   The *reference* field of the page table is used by *__page replacement algorithms__*.

F76   The *__modified__* field of the page table is used to decide if a page is selected for replacement should be written on disk.

F77   The leftover space when a process gets more memory than its requirement, is called *__internal fragmentation__*.

F78   The condition when a referenced page number is not present in the TLB is called *__TLB miss__*.

F79   Every reference to a data (in the worst case) has two memory accesses – one access for *__the page table__*, and the other for *__the actual data__*.

F80   The hash values in the entries of a hashed page table correspond to *__logical (virtual) page numbers__*.

F81   The maximum logical address that the CPU is allowed to access is contained in the *__limit__* register.

F82   The dynamic storage-allocation algorithm which results in the smallest leftover hole in memory is *__best fit__*.

F83   The dynamic storage-allocation algorithm which results in the largest leftover hole in memory is *__worst fit__*.

F84   A(n) *__inverted__* page table has one page entry for each frame of memory (RAM).

F85   With a page size of 8 KB, the number of bits required to represent the byte offset in the logical address is **13**.

F86   The number of entries in the page table where 18 bits of a logical address represent an entry in the page table, is **262144**.

F87   With segmentation, a logical address consists of **_segment number_** and **_offset_**.

F88   The location of segment table in memory is in **_segment-table base register (STBR)_**.

F89   The number of segments used by a program is in **_segment-table length register (STLR)_**.

F90   The condition when a process spends more time paging than executing is called **_thrashing_**.

F91   Swapping out is the processes of moving a page from **_main memory_** to **_disk_**.

F92   The situation where there is enough total memory space, but the available space is not contiguous to satisfy a request, is called **_external fragmentation_**.

F93   A segment is spread across several pages in the **_paged segmented_** memory management system.

F94   Use of combinations of main memory (RAM) and disk storage to provide each process a view of a large contiguous space is called **_virtual memory_**.

F95   Recent translations of virtual memory to physical memory are stored in **_translation look-aside buffer (TLB)_**.

F96   Bringing pages into memory frames (based on prediction) even before they are accessed is called **_prepaging_**.

F97   The **_modify_** bit is useful in making page replacement efficient.

F98   The page number corresponds to the **_higher_** order bits of the logical address.

F99   The **_protection_** bits in a page table entry indicate the kinds of permissible operations on the page.

F100   The inverted page table is **_smaller_** than the (normal) page table.

F101   The contents of the entries in segment table are **_base_** and **_limit_**.

F102 The ***modified (dirty)*** bit is useful when a page is selected for replacement.

F103 The ***OPT page replacement*** algorithm, although not implementable, is used for assessing performance of other page-replacement schemes.

F104 The table in main memory which contains segment information, including the segment number and its corresponding memory address, is called ***segment map table***.

F105 A ***fixed partition*** scheme requires that the entire program be stored contiguously.

F106 In a ***dynamic partition*** scheme programs may be relocated to different parts of memory.

F107 The highest location in memory accessible by a program is stored in ***bounds register***.

F108 The starting address of a process in memory is stored in the ***relocation register***.

F109 Loading only a part of the program into memory as required is called ***demand paging***.

F110 Using the page that has been in memory the longest as candidate for removal is used in ***first-in first-out (FIFO)*** page replacement algorithm.

F111 The page replacement algorithm that is often used in practice is the ***least recently used (LRU)***.

F112 The four factors in the design of cache memory are ***cache size***, ***block (cache line) size***, ***block replacement algorithm***, and ***rewrite policy***.

F113 The two major cache rewrite policies are ***write-through*** and ***write-back***.

F114 A memory allocation scheme in which jobs are given as much memory as they request when they are loaded for processing, is called ***dynamic partition***.

F115   ***Page numbers*** are used as indices to look up the page table to get corresponding physical frames.

F116   In a 2 level paging system with 10 bits each for page address and 12 bits for the offset, the page size is **4KB**.

F117   In a 2 level paging system with 32-bit virtual address, first-level page address of 10 bits, and a page size of 4KB, the number of page tables at level 1 is **1**.

F118   In a 2 level paging system with 32-bit virtual address, 12 bits for first-level page address, and a page size of 1KB, the number of page tables at level 2 is **1024**.

F119   The mechanism which enables execution of programs larger than can fit in memory (RAM) is called ***virtual memory***.

F120   Physical memory is divided into equal sized units called ***frames***.

F121   Virtual memory is divided into equal sized units called ***pages***.

F122   The bit in the page table entry used to indicate whether the page is valid (*i.e.* currently in memory) or not is called ***valid bit***.

F123   The problem of a large and sparse page table resulting from a large virtual address space is solved by having a(n) ***inverted page table (or hashed page table)***.

F124   A TLB with added process identifiers to the TLB lines is called ***tagged TLB***.

F125   A ***lazy swapper*** swaps a page into memory only if that page is needed.

F126   An *offset* in the logical address which is greater than the *limit* field of the segment table entry generates a ***trap***.

F127   Increasing the number of page frames in main memory could resulting in increased page faults under FIFO page replacement is referred to as ***Belady's*** anomaly.

F128   The worst case number of page faults that can occur in the execution of an instruction which reads two variables, does an operation on them, and writes the result to another variable, is **4** (one each for instruction read, two data reads, and one data write).

F129   When a program uses only a small portion of its virtual address space a **_hashed_** page table is preferred.

F130   Under-allocation of the minimum number of pages required by a process causes **_trashing_**.

F131   A very low CPU utilization and a high disk usage is indicative of **_trashing_**.

F132   A string of referenced page numbers is called **_reference string_**.

F133   The number of entries in a conventional page table in a system with 32-bit logical address and a page size of 4 KB, is $\underline{\mathbf{2^{32} / 2^{12} = 2^{20}}}$.

F134   Given a system with M memory frames (initially empty) and a reference string of length R containing P ($> M$) distinct page numbers, the *minimum* possible number of page faults is $\underline{\boldsymbol{P}}$.

F135   Given a system with M memory frames (initially empty) and a reference string of length R, the *maximum* possible number of page faults is $\underline{\boldsymbol{R}}$.

F136   Given a system with M memory frames (initially empty) and a reference string of length R, the *minimum* number of distinct page numbers in the reference string which results in the *maximum* possible number of page faults is $\underline{\boldsymbol{M + 1}}$.

F137   The effective memory access time in a system with a TLB hit ratio of $h\%$, TLB access time of t_1 units, and main memory access time of t_2 units, is $\underline{\boldsymbol{h/100\ (t_1 + t_2) + (1 - h/100)(t_1 + 2t_2)}}$.

Note: On a TLB miss, the page table has to be accessed followed by the data access, requiring 2 memory accesses.

F138   Given a system with a cache access time of 3 nS, main memory access time of 75 nS, in order to have the effective memory access time to be less than 9 nS, the least cache hit ratio required is $\underline{\mathbf{0.92}}$. ($T_e = 9$; $T_m = 75$; $T_c = 3$; Use $T_e = T_c + (1 - h)\, T_m\ < 9$)

F139   Given a system with a cache with access time of 5 nS and a hit ratio of 0.95, to achieve effective memory access time to be no more than 10 nS, the required main memory access time should be at most **100 nS**.

F140   The optimum page size in a system with average process size of S bytes and each page table entry of E bytes, is **$\sqrt{(2SE)}$**.

F141   The average page access time in a system with a page hit ratio of 0.7, main memory access time of a page of 10 ns and secondary memory access time of a page of 1 millisecond, is **307 ns**.

F142   The number of pages in a system with page size of 8 KB and a 48-bit virtual address, is **$2^{48}/2^{13} = 2^{35}$**

F143   Of the two memory (RAM) accesses required for any instruction or data access, one is for ***the page table*** (to get the frame number), and the other for the ***actual instruction/data***.

F144   The minimum possible number of pages of a process of N pages that could be resident in main memory (at any point) during the execution of the process is **0**.

F145   The maximum possible number of pages of a process of N pages that could be resident in main memory (at any point) during the execution of the process is **N**.

F146   The minimum possible number of pages of a process of N pages that are brought into main memory (at some point) before the process finishes execution of is **1**.

F147   The minimum possible number of pages of a process of N pages that could have been swapped out (at any point) during its execution is **0**.

F148   In a byte addressable system with V bits of virtual (logical) address, a page size of P bytes, and M pages of a process in memory, the number of entries with valid bits not set in the page table is **$(2^V / P) - M$**.

F149   Given a byte addressable system with V bits of virtual address, a page size of P bytes, and a process with a total of N pages, out of which M are in memory, the number of entries with valid bits set in the page table is **M**.

F150   Given a physical memory of M frames (initially all empty) and the page-reference string of length P, with N ($> M$) *distinct* page numbers occurring in it, the minimum number of page faults is $\underline{N}$.

F151   Given a physical memory of M frames (initially all empty) and the page-reference string of length P ($> M$), the maximum possible number of page faults is $\underline{P}$.

F152   In a demand-page system with probability of a page fault of p, memory access time of t, and page-fault handling time of f, the effective access time is $\underline{(1-p) \cdot t + p \cdot f}$.

F153   In a system with M bytes of virtual address space, page size of K bytes, and each page table entry of P bytes, the size of the page table, is $\underline{(M / K) \cdot P}$.

F154   In a system with N bits in the page table entry to hold the frame number, and page size of K bytes, the physical memory (RAM) size is $\underline{2^N \cdot K\ bytes}$.

F155   In a system with a TLB hit ratio of 90%, TLB access time of 20 nS, and main memory access time of 100 nS, the effective memory access time is $\underline{130\ nS}$.

F156   In a system with a TLB hit ratio of 95%, TLB access time of 10 nS, and main memory access time of 120 nS, the effective memory access time is $\underline{136\ nS}$.

F157   In a system with a TLB hit ratio of 90%, TLB access time of 15 nS, and main memory access time of 85 nS, the effective memory access time is $\underline{108.5\ nS}$.

F158   In a system with TLB access time of 15 nS and main memory access time of 100 nS, the TLB hit ratio required to achieve an effective memory access time of 120 nS, is $\underline{0.95}$.

F159   In a system with main memory access time of 250 nS and a cache hit ratio of 95%, the cache access time required to have average memory access time of 32.5 nS, is $\underline{20\ nS}$.

F160   In a system with 32-bit virtual addresses, page size of 4 KB, a 4-way set associative translation look-aside buffer (TLB) of 128 entries, the number of bits in the TLB tag is $\underline{15\ bits}$.

F161   In a system with 32-bit virtual addresses, page size of 4 KB, a 4-way set associative translation look-aside buffer (TLB) of 64 entries, the number of bits in the TLB tag is **16 *bits***.

F162   Given the logical address 0xAB76 (in hexadecimal) with a page size of 256 bytes, the page number is **0xAB**.

F163   Given the logical address 0xAE9C (in hexadecimal) with a page size of 256 bytes, the offset within the page is **0x9C**.

F164   Given the logical address 0xAB76 (in hexadecimal) with a page size of 1024 bytes, the page number is **0x2A**.

F165   Given the logical address 0xAB76 (in hexadecimal) with a page size of 1024 bytes, the offset within the page is **0x376**.

F166   Given the logical address 0xAE9C (in hexadecimal) with a page size of 1024 bytes, the page number is **0x29C**.

F167   Given the logical address 0xAE9C (in hexadecimal) with a page size of 1024 bytes, the offset within the page is **0x2B**.

F168   In a two-level paging system with an 8 KB page size, and a 32-bit logical address, and the outer page table with 1024 entries, the number of bits are used to represent the second-level page table is **9**.

F169   In a system with average main memory (RAM) access time of 250 nS, and average cache access time of 30 nS, the *cache hit ratio* required to have an average memory access time of at least 50 nS, is **92%**.

F170   A(n) ***process identifier*** matches the process with each entry in the TLB.

F171   The ***bounds*** register is used to check for invalid memory addresses generated by a CPU.

F172   The *minimum* possible number of page faults for a process with 10 pages, and 4 main memory frames, with all the pages being accessed during the execution of the process, is **10**.

F173   The *maximum* possible number of page faults for a process with 10 pages, and 4 main memory frames, and 17 references to pages during the execution of the process, is **17**.

F174   In a system with 3 main memory frames, and a process referencing pages in the order: *A, C, C, B, A, D, F, E, F, F, G, F, D, A, B*, the *hit ratio* using *FIFO* page replacement algorithm is **5 / 15**.

F175   In a system with 3 main memory frames, and a process referencing pages in the order: *A, C, C, B, A, D, F, E, F, F, G, F, D, A, B*, the final content of the frames using *FIFO* page replacement algorithm is ***A, B, D***.

F176   In a system with 3 main memory frames, and a process referencing pages in the order: *A, C, C, B, A, D, F, E, F, F, G, F, D, A, B*, the *hit ratio* using *LRU* page replacement algorithm is **5 / 15**.

F177   In a system with 3 main memory frames, and a process referencing pages in the order: *A, C, C, B, A, D, F, E, F, F, G, F, D, A, B*, the final content of the frames using *LRU* page replacement algorithm is ***D, A, B***.

F178   In a system with 3 main memory frames, and a process referencing pages in the order: *A, C, C, B, A, D, F, E, F, F, G, F, D, A, B*, the *hit ratio* using *OPT* page replacement algorithm is **6 / 15**.

F179   In a system with 3 main memory frames, and a process referencing pages in the order: *A, C, A, B, B, E, A, F, B*, the *hit ratio* using *FIFO* page replacement algorithm is **2 / 9**.

F180   In a system with 3 main memory frames, and a process referencing pages in the order: *A, C, A, B, B, E, A, F, B*, the final content of the frames using *FIFO* page replacement algorithm is ***B, A, F***.

F181   In a system with 3 main memory frames, and a process referencing pages in the order: *A, C, A, B, B, E, A, F, B*, the *hit ratio* using *LRU* page replacement algorithm is **3 / 9**.

F182   In a system with 3 main memory frames, and a process referencing pages in the order: *A, C, A, B, B, E, A, F, B*, the final content of the frames using *LRU* page replacement algorithm is ***A, B, F***.

F183   In a system with 3 main memory frames, and a process referencing pages in the order: *A, C, A, B, B, E, A, F, B,* the *hit ratio* using *OPT* page replacement algorithm is **4 / 9**.

F184   The size of a process which requires four 256-byte pages with a fragmentation of 55 bytes, is **4 · 256 – 55 = 969 *bytes***.

F185   The fragmentation of a process with a size of 1500 Bytes if the page size is 256 bytes, is **256 · 6 – 1500 = 36 *bytes***.

F186   The size of a process which uses six 256–byte pages and has the minimum fragmentation, is **256 · 6 =1536 *bytes***.

F187   The size of a process which uses four 256–byte pages and has the maximum fragmentation, is **256 · 3 + 1 = 769 *bytes***.

F188   In a system with a page size of 256 bytes, the number of pages required for a process of 2000 bytes, is **⌈2000 / 256⌉ = 8**.

F189   In a system with a page size of 256 bytes, the page number where an item with byte address 925 be located, is **⌊925 / 256⌋ = 3**.

F190   In a system with a page size of 256 bytes, the size of a program which requires 4 pages and has a fragmentation of 45 bytes, is **256 · 4 – 45 = 979 *bytes***.

F191   In a system with a page size of 256 bytes, the fragmentation of a process with a size of 1600 bytes is **256 · 7 – 1600 = 192**.

F192   In a system with a page size of 256 bytes, the displacement (offset) of an item with a byte address of 342 is **342 *MOD* 256 = 86**

F193   In a paged memory system with a page size of 512 bytes, the number of pages required for a process of size 4,000 bytes, is **⌈4000 / 512)⌉ = 8**.

F194   In a system with a page size of 512 bytes, the fragmentation (unused bytes) for a process of size 4,000 bytes, is **8 · 512 – 4000 = 96 bytes**.

F195   In a system with a page size of 512 bytes, for a process of size 4,000 bytes, the page which holds an item located at byte number 2020 of the process (page 0 being the first page), is **page 3**.

F196   In a paged memory system with a page size of 512 bytes, the size of a process which takes up 5 pages and leaves unused space of 300 bytes, is **$4 \cdot 512 + 212 = 2260$ *bytes***.

F197   In a paged memory system with a page size of 512 bytes, the page that holds an item located at byte number 800 of a process, (page 0 being the first page), is **page 1**.

F198   If the system can allocate all resources requested by all processes (up to their stated maximums) without entering a deadlock state, it is said to be in ***a safe state***.

F199   In a K-level hierarchy of paging, the number of memory accesses (in the worst case) to access a data item is **$K + 1$**.

F200   The number of bits in the memory address for a main memory size of 4GB is **32 bits (since $4GB = 2^{32}$)**.

F201   The number of frames in a main memory size of 4GB with a frame size of 2KB is **$2^{20} = 2M = 2{,}097{,}152$**.

F202   In a system with 32-bit virtual address and main memory frame size of 2 KB, the number of page table entries is **$2^{32} / 2^{11} = 2^{21} = 2M$**.

F203   In a system with 20-bit physical address, and a frame size of 1 KB, the number of main memory frames is **$2^{20} / 2^{10} = 2^{10} = 1024$**.

F204   Given a logical address space of 4GB, a page table with 2M entries, and a physical memory of 256 MB, the number of bits in logical address is **32**.

F205   Given a logical address space of 4GB, a page table with 2M entries, and a physical memory of 256 MB, the number of bits in physical address is **28**.

F206   Given a logical address space of 4GB, a page table with 2M entries, and a physical memory of 256 MB, the number of bits of address required to index a page is **21**, and to index a frame is **17**.

F207   Given that logical address consists of 16 bits and the page size is 512 bytes, the number of pages is **128**.

F208 In a system with a logical address of 20 bits and 2K pages, the page size is **512 _bytes_**.

F209 In a system with a physical memory of 256 frames, each of size 1024 bytes, the number of bits in the physical address is **18**.

F210 Given that a page table entry has 15 bits for frame number, and a main memory frame size is 2048 bytes the size of main memory is $2^{15} \cdot 2^{11} = 2^{15}$ **_bytes_**.

F211 In a system with a physical memory frame size of 4KB and 4096 _entries_ in the page table, the number of bits of logical address is **24**.

F212 In a system with a 128MB virtual address space and a physical memory frame size of 2KB, the number of _entries_ in the page table is $2^{27} / 2^{11} = 2^{18} =$ **256K**.

F213 In a system with a page size of 2 KB, the number of bits in the logical address required to denote the offset within a page is **11**.

F214 Given that a logical address consists of 16 bits and the page size is 512 bytes, the number of pages is **128**.

F215 In a (byte addressable) system with a logical address of 20 bits and 4096 pages, the page size is **256 _bytes_**.

F216 Given that a system has 8K pages and each page is 2K bytes, the number of bits in the logical address is **24**.

F217 Given that the physical memory has 256 frames, each of size 1024 bytes, the bits in the physical address is **18**.

F218 Given that a page table has 1024 entries and each entry has 9 bits for a frame number, the number of frames of physical memory is $2^{10} \times 2^9 = 2^{19} =$ **512K**.

F219 In a (byte addressable) system with a logical address of 20 bits and 2048 pages, the page size is **512 _bytes_**.

F220 In a system with 2048 pages, the number of bits for byte offset within a page of 9 bits, the size of logical address space is $2^{20} =$ **1M _bytes_**.

F221   In a system with 2048 pages, main memory of 256 frames, the size of the page table assuming 4 status bits, is **$2048 \cdot (8 + 4)$ _bits_ = 3072 _bytes_**.

F222   In a system with a physical memory of 256 frames, each of size 512 bytes, the number of bits in the physical address is **17**.

F223   Given that the logical address is 32 bits, and the page size is 4096 bytes, the number of pages is **$2^{32} / 2^{12} = 2^{20} = 1$ M $(1,024 \cdot 1,024)$**.

F224   Given that the page size is 4096 bytes and 256 frames in the main memory, the number of bits in the physical address is **$14 + 8 = 20$**.

F225   Given that a system has virtual memory space of 2^{32} bytes, and page size is 4096 bytes, the number of page table entries is **$2^{32} / 2^{12} = 2^{20}$**.

F226   Given a page size of 4 KB, the number of bits required for the page offset in the logical address is **12**.

F227   In a (byte addressable) system with a 24 bits logical address and 4096 pages, the page size is **4096 _bytes_**.

F228   In a system with 2048 pages and each page of size 512 bytes, the number of bits in logical address is **20**.

F229   In a system with a logical address space of 4GB, and a page size of 4KB, the number of bits for indexing a page is **20**.

F230   In a system with a physical memory of 4K frames, each of size 1K bytes, the number of bits in the physical address is **22**.

F231   In a 64-bit machine, with 2 GB RAM, and 8 KB page size, the number of entries in the inverted page table is **2^{18} $(= 2^{31}/2^{13})$**.

F232   In a system with a page size of 512 bytes, each page table entry having 11 bits for the frame number, the physical memory size is **$2^{20} = 1$M _bytes_**.

F233   For a process with N pages, the number of entries in the page table is **N**.

F234   For a process with N pages, each page of P bytes, the size of the process is **$N \cdot P$ _bytes_**.

F235   In a system with N bits of physical address, and a page size of P bytes, the number of entries in the inverted page table is **$2^N / P$**.

F236   Given a virtual address of 32 bits and a page size of 4KB, the number of bits in the address for the page number is **20**.

F237   Given a virtual address of 32 bits and, the number of bits in the physical address for offset within a frame of 11 bits, the number of pages is **$2M\ (2^{22})$**.

F238   Given a virtual address of 32 bits and 22 bits in the physical address for the page number, the page size is **1KB**.

F239   Given a system with a main memory size of 4GB, cache size of 1 MB, and a cache line size of 64 bytes, the number of cache lines, is **$1MB / 64B = 2^{20} / 2^6 = 2^{14} = 16K$**.

F240   Given a system with a main memory size of 4GB, cache size of 1 MB, and a cache line size of 64 bytes, the possible number of memory blocks that would map to a given cache line using direct mapping, is **4K** (No. of memory blocks / No. of cache lines = $2^{26} / 2^{14} = 2^{12}$)

F241   Given a system with a main memory size of 4GB, cache size of 1 MB, and a cache line size of 64 bytes, the size of the cache tag, assuming a fully associative mapping, is **26**. (Number of bits for byte offset within a block (line) = 6; Number of tag bits = 32 – 6 = 26)

F242   Given a system with a main memory size of 4GB, cache size of 1 MB, and a cache line size of 64 bytes, the size of the cache tag, assuming a 4-way associative mapping, the number of bits for addressing a set is **12**. (No. of sets = No. of cache lines / No. of lines per set = $2^{14} / 2^2 = 2^{12}$)

F243   Given a system with a main memory size of 4GB, cache size of 1 MB, and a cache line size of 64 bytes, the size of the cache tag, assuming a 4-way associative mapping, the number of tag bits is **14**. (32–6–12)

F244   In a paged memory system with a page size of 512 bytes, the size of a process requiring 5 pages, and having a fragmentation of 200 bytes, is **$4 \cdot 512 + 312 = 2360\ bytes$**.

F245   Given five memory partitions M_1 to M_5 of 100 KB, 450 KB, 250 KB, 300 KB, and 500 KB, and four processes P_1 to P_4 with memory requirements of 210 KB, 325 KB, 127 KB, and 432 KB, the assignment of processes to partitions using *first-fit* allocation is **$P_1 \rightarrow M_2$; $P_2 \rightarrow M_5$; $P_3 \rightarrow M_2$; P_4 cannot be allocated**.

F246   Given five memory partitions M_1 to M_5 of 100 KB, 450 KB, 250 KB, 300 KB, and 500 KB, and four processes P_1 to P_4 with memory requirements of 210 KB, 325 KB, 127 KB, and 432 KB, the assignment of processes to partitions using *best-fit* allocation is **$P_1 \rightarrow M_3$; $P_2 \rightarrow M_2$; $P_3 \rightarrow M_4$; $P_4 \rightarrow M_5$**.

F247   Given five memory partitions M_1 to M_5 of 100 KB, 450 KB, 250 KB, 300 KB, and 500 KB, and four processes P_1 to P_4 with memory requirements of 210 KB, 325 KB, 127 KB, and 432 KB, the assignment of processes to partitions using *worst-fit* allocation is **$P_1 \rightarrow M_5$; $P_2 \rightarrow M_2$; $P_3 \rightarrow M_4$; P_4 cannot be allocated**.

F248   Given a system with a 1 KB page size, and the address 2563 (given as decimal numbers), the corresponding page number is **2** and the offset is **515**. (2563 DIV 1024 = 2; 2563 MOD 1024 = 515)

F249   Given a system with a 1 KB page size, and the address 18967 (given as decimal numbers), the corresponding page number is **18** and the offset is **535**. (18967 DIV 1024 = 18; 18967 MOD 1024 = 535)

F250   Given a logical address space of 64 pages and 1024 bytes per page, mapped onto a physical memory of 16 frames, the number of bits required in the logical address is **16** and the number of bits required in the physical address is **14**.

F251   The fields in each node of the linked list in each entry of the hashed page table are ***virtual page number***, ***value of the mapped page frame***, and ***pointer to the next node in the linked list***.

F252   The effective instruction time in a system with (average) instruction execution time of I units, (average) page fault handling time of J units, and average page fault rate of one every K instructions, is **$I + J / K$**.

F253   The context switch overhead time for swapping out a 50 MB process and bringing in a 25 MB process, with a disk transfer rate of 50 MB per second, and average disk latency of 4 milliseconds, is **1.508 sec**.

F254   Given F is the page fault rate (%), H is the page hit rate (%), T is the time to service a page fault, and M is the memory access time, the *average memory access time* is $\underline{\mathbf{(F{\cdot}T + H{\cdot}M) / 100}}$.

F255   Given that a system has two cache options: (a) with access time of 3 ns and a hit ratio of 0.96, and (b) with access time of 3.5ns and a hit ratio of 0.97, the upper bound on the memory access time when option (b) is beneficial, is **50 ns**.
[$T_a = 3 + (1 - 0.96)\ T_m$; $T'_a = 3.5 + (1 - 0.97)\ T_m$. For option (b) to be beneficial, $T_a > T'_a \rightarrow 3 + (1 - 0.96)T_m > 3.5 + (1 - 0.97)T_m \rightarrow 3 + 0.04T_m > 3.5 + 0.03T_m \rightarrow 0.01\ T_m > 0.5 \rightarrow T_m > 50$]

F256   The (byte addressable) logical address space corresponding to V bits of logical address is $\underline{\mathbf{2^V\ bytes}}$.

F257   In a system with V bits of logical address and a page size of 2^K bytes, the number of bits in the logical address used for the page number is $\underline{\mathbf{V - K}}$.

F258   In a system with V bits of logical address and 2^P pages, the number of bits in the logical address used for indexing a byte within a page is $\underline{\mathbf{V - P}}$.

F259   In a system with logical address space of 2^V bytes and K lower order bits in the logical address used for byte offset within a page, the number of pages is $\underline{\mathbf{2^V / 2^K = 2^{V-K}}}$.

F260   In a (byte addressable) system with V bits of logical address out of which P bits are for page number, the page size is $\underline{\mathbf{2^{V-P}}}$.

F261   In a (byte addressable) system with V bits of logical address and K bits for a byte offset within a page, the number of pages is $\underline{\mathbf{2^{V-K}}}$.

F262   In a system with a virtual address space of 2^V bytes and page size of 2^K bytes, the number of logical pages of a process is $\underline{\mathbf{2^V / 2^K = 2^{V-K}}}$.

F263   In a system with physical address space of 2^P bytes and page size of 2^K bytes, the number of physical frames in the system is $\underline{2^P / 2^K = 2^{P-K}}$.

F264   In a system with K bits for a byte offset within a page, and 2^E bytes per page table entry, the number of page table entries is $\underline{2^K / 2^E = 2^{K-E}}$.

F265   In a system using hierarchical paging with a virtual address space of 2^V bytes, page size of 2^K bytes, and 2^E bytes per page table entry, the number of pages required to store the innermost page table entries, is $\underline{2^{V-K} / 2^{K-E} = 2^{V+E-2K}}$.

F266   In a system using hierarchical paging with $L\ (\geq 2)$ levels, a virtual address space of 2^V bytes, page size of 2^K bytes, and 2^E bytes per page table entry, L (in terms of V, K, and E) is given by $\underline{[(V-K)\,/\,(K-E)]}$.

F267   In a system using hierarchical paging with $L\ (\geq 2)$ levels, a virtual address space of 2^V bytes, page size of 2^K bytes, and 2^E bytes per page table entry, V_0 – the number of (most significant) bits of the virtual address that are used as an index into the outermost page table–is given by $\underline{V - K - (L-1) \cdot (K-E)}$.

G. I/O subsystem

G1   **Device queue** contains the list of processes waiting for a particular I/O device.

G2   The mechanism which facilitates the sharing of a printer (but not at the same time) among different processes is called **spooling**.

G3   The **I/O device handler** processes I/O interrupts and handles error conditions.

G4   Code / software to control I/O devices are in **device drivers**.

G5   The registers of the I/O devices are mapped into the memory space of the processor in **memory-mapped I/O**.

G6   The processor has special I/O instructions to control the IO device directly in **programmed I/O**.

G7   When I/O is slow or of large sizes, **interrupt-driven I/O** is more efficient.

G8   Interrupt driven I/O is more efficient than polling for **slow** I/O devices.

G9   The **I/O module** acts as the interface between the CPU and the peripheral devices.

G10   There is a single address space for memory locations and I/O devices in **memory–mapped** I/O.

G11   In **DMA** mode the I/O module and main memory exchange data directly, without processor involvement.

G12   The processor need not wait for the duration of I/O, but continue with the execution of program instructions in the **interrupt driven** mode of I/O.

G13   The CPU waiting for the I/O operation to complete, by repeatedly checking the device status is called **busy wait**.

G14   In **polling**, the CPU must periodically scan (read) an address to check if an input has arrived.

G15   The CPU accesses the device memory much like it accesses main memory in ***memory-mapped*** I/O.

G16   The inability of the CPU to do a memory access when the DMA controller is doing data transfer is called ***cycle stealing***.

G17   The *device-dependent* software for a device (or class of devices) is contained in ***device drivers***.

G18   The hardware that controls (operates) the actual device is called ***device controller (I/O controller)***.

G19   There is no explicit I/O instruction in a CPU with ***memory mapped*** I/O.

G20   When I/O completion times are known to be long, ***interrupts*** are better suited for handling I/O.

G21   The error detection in I/O operations is the responsibility of the ***I/O module***.

G22   A(n) ***I/O module*** is the interface between the CPU and the peripheral device.

G23   For CPUs having memory-mapped I/O, protection of I/O is ensured by ***operating system routine(s)***.

G24   In ***programmed I/O*** the CPU is tied up during a data transfer from the device to I/O module.

G25   When the I/O is frequent and of short duration, ***polling*** is a better I/O mechanism.

G26   The three major modes of I/O are ***programmed I/O***, ***interrupt-driven I/O***, and ***direct memory access (DMA)***.

G27   The *device driver* provides an interface between the ***device controller*** and the ***operating system***.

G28   The device controller communicates with the operating system via the ***device driver***.

G29   The hardware which operates the device is called the ***device controller***.

G30   In DMA the interrupt signaling I/O completion is sent to the CPU by the ***disk controller***.

G31   The module of the operating system responsible for controlling the use of devices is the ***Device manager***.

G32   If the processor iterates a busy-waiting loop many times before the I/O completes, use of ***interrupt*** is better than ***polling***.

G33   An I/O which does not put a process in a waiting state is called ***non-blocking* or *asynchronous*** I/O.

G34   In a system with a device generating 800 interrupts per second, and each interrupt processing consuming 100 μs, the fraction of processor time consumed for interrupt processing is **0.08**.

G35   In a system with a device generating 400 interrupts per second, and each interrupt processing consuming 120 μs, the fraction of time the processor does useful work is **0.952**.

G36   The CPU utilization in a system with N processes waiting for I/O, where a process spends a fraction p of its time in I/O wait state, is given by $\mathbf{1 - p^N}$.

H. Secondary (disk) storage and file system

H1   The module of the operating system responsible for use and operations of files is called *file manager*.

H2   The *seek time* is the longest of the times in a disk access.

H3   The *SSTF* (*shortest seek time first*) *disk* scheduling algorithm services the request which is on a track *closest* to the current R/W head position.

H4   The SSTF scheduling algorithm services the request with *the minimum seek time*.

H5   The disk scheduling algorithm where the request with the smallest seek time is serviced next is called *shortest seek time first (SSTF)*.

H6   The arm/head starts at one end of the disk, moves towards the other end, servicing requests in order until there are no more requests in that direction, then reverses direction, and services requests the other way, in the *SCAN disk scheduling* algorithm.

H7   The disk head may not fully traverse the disk in the *Look / C-Look* disk head scheduling algorithm.

H8   The mechanism where a group of disks is treated as a single unit is called *disk striping*.

H9   The surface of a magnetic disk platter is divided into concentric circular *tracks*.

H10   Each track of a magnetic disk is divided into *sectors*.

H11   The disk head scheduling algorithm which does not take into account the current position of the disk head is *FCFS*.

H12   What are the two components of positioning time of a disk head are *seek time* and *rotational latency*.

H13   A particular track number across all the platters is collectively called *cylinder*.

H14   The ***rotational latency*** component of a disk's I/O time is dependent on the disk's RPM.

H15   The tracks of a magnetic disk platter are divided into ***sectors***.

H16   A set of disk blocks that logically belong on disk, but are kept in a portion of memory to improve performance is called ***disk cache***.

H17   The swap space usually resides on the ***disk***.

H18   The disk scheduling algorithm where disk requests are serviced as they arrive is called ***FCFS***.

H19   The smallest block that can be read or written on a disk is called ***sector***.

H20   The components of a disk read/write time are ***seek time***, ***rotational latency***, and ***data transfer (read/write) time***.

H21   The ***seek time*** is the longest of the times in a disk access.

H22   Each file is a linked list of disk blocks in ***linked*** allocation.

H23   Insertion and deletion of blocks in a file is easy in ***linked*** allocation of disk blocks in a file system.

H24   Support for *very* large files is provided by ***multi-level indexed*** allocation.

H25   The ***FCFS*** disk head scheduling does not take into account the current position of the disk head.

H26   The scheme for deciding the order in which disk access requests are serviced is called ***disk scheduling***.

H27   A set of physical disk drives viewed as a single logical unit by the OS is called ***RAID (redundant array of independent disks)***.

H28   The number of RAID levels are numbered ***level 0*** to ***level 6***.

H29   Blocks level striping, but without any redundancy (parity) is used in RAID level ***0***.

H30   Disk mirroring is used in RAID level ***1***.

H31   Striping at the level of bytes is used in RAID level **2**.

H32   Bit-interleaved parity organization is used in RAID level **3**.

H33   Block-interleaved parity organization is used in RAID level **4**.

H34   A separate disk for parity for the blocks from other disks is used in RAID level **4**.

H35   Block-interleaved distributed parity is used in RAID level **5**.

H36   Block-level interleaving is used in RAID levels **4** and **5**.

H37   Multiple disk failures is handled in RAID level **6**.

H38   For each block, one of the disks stores the parity and the others store data in RAID level **5**.

H39   Error-correcting codes (such as the Reed-Solomon codes) are used in RAID level **6**.

H40   The average *rotational latency* ($\frac{1}{2}$ of the time in seconds for one rotation the disk) of a disk drive with 7,200 RPM (rotations per minute) is **4.165 *milliseconds***.

H41   The number of bytes in a *cylinder* of a disk drive with 5 platters, each with 2 surfaces, 27,000 tracks per surface, 512 sectors per track, and 512 bytes per sector, is **$10 \cdot 512 \cdot 512$ *bytes***.

H42   Given a disk queue holding requests to the following cylinders (tracks) **116,22,3,11,75,185,100,87**, in order, and that the disk head is currently at cylinder (track) 88, using FCFS, the total head movement (no. of tracks traversed) is **421**, and the average head movement is **52.625**.

H43   Given a disk queue holding requests to the following cylinders (tracks) **116,22,3,11,75,185,100,87**, in order, and that the disk head is currently at cylinder (track) 88, using SSTF (shortest seek time first), the total head movement (number of tracks traversed) is **305**, and the average head movement is **38.125**.

H44   Given a disk queue holding requests to the following cylinders (tracks) **116,22,3,11,75,185,100,87**, in order, and that the disk head is currently at cylinder (track) 88, using SSTF (shortest seek time first), the order in which the requests are serviced is **87,75,100,116,185,22,11,3**.

H45   Given a disk queue holding requests to the following cylinders (tracks) **116,22,3,11,75,185,100,87**, in order, and that the disk head is currently at cylinder (track) 88, using C-SCAN, the total head movement (no. of tracks traversed) is **363**, and the average head movement is **45.375**.

H46   Given a disk queue holding requests to the following cylinders (tracks) **116,22,3,11,75,185,100,87**, in order, and that the disk head is currently at cylinder (track) 88, using C-SCAN, the order in which the requests are serviced is **100,116,185, (end) 3,11,22,75,87**.

H47   In constant linear velocity disk drive, the density of track is **_uniform_** going from outer tracks to inner tracks.

H48   In constant angular velocity disk drive, the density of track is **_increasing_** going from the **_outer_** tracks to the **_inner_** tracks.

IOIOIOIOIOIOIOIOIOIOIOIOIOIOIOIOIOIOIOIOIOIOIOIOIOIOIOIOI

Books on Operating Systems

- Avi Silberschatz, Peter Galvin, and Greg Gagne. *Operating System Concepts* (9th Edition). John Wiley & Sons, 2013. ISBN-13: 978-1118063330

- Andrew S. Tanenbaum and Herbert Bos. *Modern Operating Systems* (4th Edition). Pearson, 2014. ISBN-13: 978-0133591620.

- William Stallings. *Operating Systems: Internals and Design Principles* (9th Edition). Pearson, 2017. ISBN-13: 978-0134670959.

- Douglas Comer. *Operating System Design: The Xinu Approach*, (2nd Edition). Chapman and Hall/CRC, 2015. ISBN-13: 978-1498712439.

- Charles Crowley. *Operating Systems: A Design-Oriented Approach*. Richard Irwin, 1996. ISBN-13: 9780256151510.

- Gary J. Nutt. *Operating Systems: A Modern Perspective*. Addison-Wesley, 1997. ISBN-13: 978-0805312959.

- J. Archer Harris and John Cordani. *Operating Systems*. McGraw-Hill (Schaum's Outline Series) 2002. ISBN-13: 978-0071364355.

Other Related Quiz Books

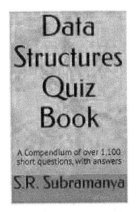

Data Structures Quiz Book

A Compendium of over 1,100 short questions, with answers

S.R. Subramanya

This is a quick assessment book / quiz book. It has a vast collection of over 1,100 questions, with answers on Data Structures. Questions have a wide range of difficulty levels and are designed to test a thorough understanding of the topical material. The coverage includes elementary and advanced data structures – **Arrays (single/multidimensional); Linked lists (singly–linked, doubly–linked, circular); Stacks; Queues; Heaps; Hash tables; Binary trees; Binary search trees; Balanced trees (AVL trees, Red–Black trees, B–trees/B+ trees); Graphs.**

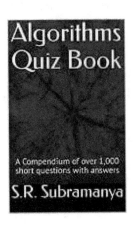

Algorithms Quiz Book

A Compendium of over 1,000 short questions with answers

S.R. Subramanya

This is a quick assessment book / quiz book. It has a vast collection of over 1,000 questions, with answers on Algorithms. The book **covers questions on standard (classical) algorithm design techniques; sorting and searching; graph traversals; minimum spanning trees; shortest path problems; maximum flow problems;** elementary concepts in P and NP Classes. It also covers a few specialized areas – string processing; polynomial operations; numerical & matrix computations; computational geometry & computer graphics

Computer Security Quiz Book

A Compendium of over 1,700 short questions with answers

S.R. Subramanya

This is a quick assessment book / quiz book. It has a wide variety of over 1,700 questions, with answers on Computer Security. The questions have a wide range of difficulty levels and are designed to test a thorough understanding of the topical material. The book covers all the major topics in a typical first course in Computer Security – Cryptography, Authentication and Key Management, Software and Operating Systems Security, Malware, Attacks, Network Security, and Web Security.

This is a quick assessment book / quiz book. It has wide variety of ~1,400 questions on Programming Languages and Compilers. It covers questions on: Bindings and Scopes, Data types, Expressions and Assignment statements, Subprograms and Parameter passing mechanisms, Abstract Data Types, Object-Oriented constructs, and Exception handling. The topics related to Compilers include programming language syntax and semantics, lexical analysis, parsing, and different parsing techniques.

This is a quick assessment book / quiz book. It has a vast collection of over 1,200 short questions, with answers and programs, on Java programming language. The topical coverage includes data types, control structures, arrays, classes, objects, and methods, inheritance and polymorphism, exception handling, and stream and text I/O

This is a quick assessment book / quiz book. It has a vast collection of over 1,000 short questions, with answers and programs, on C++ programming language. The topical coverage includes data types, control structures, arrays, pointers and reference, classes and objects, inheritance and polymorphism, exception handling, and stream and text I/O.

This is a quick assessment book / quiz book. It has a vast collection of over 1,100 short questions, with answers and programs, on C programming language. It covers all the major topics of C programming – data types, operators, expressions, control structures, pointers, arrays, structures, unions, enumerated types, functions, dynamic storage management, I/O and Library functions.

This is a quick assessment book / quiz book. It has a vast collection of over 1,500 short questions, with answers. It covers all the major topics in a typical first course in Computer Networks. The coverage includes, the various layers of the Internet (TCP/IP) protocol stack (going from the actual transmission of signals to the applications that users use) – physical layer, data link layer, network layer, transport layer, and application layer, network security, and Web security.

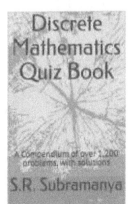

This is a self–assessment / quiz /exercise book. It has a vast collection of over 1,200 questions, with solutions, in Discrete Mathematics. Questions have a wide range of difficulty levels and are designed to test a thorough understanding of the topical material. The topical coverage includes: Logic and Proof methods, Sets, Functions, Relations, Properties of integers, Sequences, Induction and Recursion, Basic and advanced counting methods, Discrete probability, Graph theory, Modeling computation, and Boolean algebra.

www.ingramcontent.com/pod-product-compliance
Lightning Source LLC
LaVergne TN
LVHW051440050326
832903LV00030BD/3174

* 9 7 9 8 6 6 9 9 8 0 8 1 8 *